Forever God

The Loving Light Books Series

Also by Liane Rich

Loving Light

Book 9

Forever God

Liane Rich

The information contained in this book is not intended as a substitute for professional medical advice. Neither the publisher nor the author is engaged in rendering professional advice to the reader. The remedies and suggestions in this book should not be taken, or construed, as standard medical diagnosis, prescription or treatment. For any medical issue or illness consult a qualified physician.

Loving Light Books
Original Copyright © 1992
Copyright © 2009 Liane

ISBN 13: 978-1-878480-09-5
ISBN 10: 1-878480-09-X

Loving Light Books:
www.lovinglightbooks.com

Also Available at:
Amazon: www.amazon.com
Barnes & Noble: www.barnesandnoble.com

for Jack N.

The information in this series is not necessarily meant to be taken literally. It is meant to *shift* your consciousness....

Foreword

Anyone immersed in the vast body of new metaphysical knowledge is aware of the virtual symphony of voices from channeled sources throughout the world – inspirational voices that may be artistic, poetic, philosophical, religious, or scientific. And now, out of these myriad New Age voices, comes a series of books by God, channeled through Liane, revealing the frank truth in all its glory and wonder, telling us how to cleanse our bodies, gain access to our subconscious minds, clear our other selves and march back to who we are – God.

In God's books you will be introduced to a loving, powerful, gripping, exciting, and often humorous voice that reaches out and speaks ever so personally to the individual reader. As the reader's interest deepens, invariably an intimate relationship to this voice develops. It is a relationship that lasts forever, and I am quite certain I do mean forever.

Here is an accelerated program, a no-holds-barred course, where God guides us and loves us, and as needs be recommends books to us and even a movie or musical piece along the way. He (She) enters our lives and sees through our eyes, seeming to enjoy the ride as He guides us back to US, back to ALL. Here is a voice that is playful and informative, that is humorous and serious, that is gentle and powerfully divine. It is a voice that knows no barriers or restrictions, a straightforward and honest voice that caresses us when we need the warmth and pushes us when we are immobilized.

In today's New Age literature there is an avalanche of information from magnificent beings of light, information that possesses us and compels us to look at our fears and express our love. In this series of books by God, you will find truly powerful methods for making this transition from toxicity to purity, from density to light, from fear to love, and from the delusion of death to the awakening to full life. You will experience in these books the love and the power of God for it is your love to express and your power to behold. Rarely will you see more lucid steps for transformation. Read these beautiful words and rejoice in our period of awakening, our return to Home.

John Farrell, PhD., LCSW. — Psychologist, Clinical Social Worker, Senior Clinician Psychiatric Emergency Services, U.C. Davis Medical Center, Sacramento. John is also a retired Professor — California State University, Sacramento, in Health Sciences and Psychology.

Forever God

Introduction

Now I will begin to show you how you too may come to love and be loved. Most of you have a great deal of love; you just don't know how to see it. It is you. It is all the parts of you that you don't know exist. Once I told you that I am the plasma in your blood, I am the stuff you are made of. You each carry large quantities of God and these are what keep you in God. You are part of what *is* the general makeup of God. You are the being who became matter in order to experience a reversal of what you are.

Now; when you begin to unwind and shift down, you will see how you do not become God in an instant. You *are* the birth of God and you are being born at this very moment. Birth is simply a coming out in this material plane. You will come out and you will know that you are God in matter. You will de-densify and raise matter to a new level. This is the second coming that is so often talked about. You will raise your level of vibration until you no longer *feel* like man. You will *feel* like God and you will *know* that you have created your own birth.

11

Now; when you begin to rise up, you will begin to feel many pulls – as gravity is a strong *belief* here on earth. So, as you ascend to your next level of thinking you may be pulled at to stay down or stay put. This will create a feeling of pain or loss. Some of your current friends may not be ready to accept this new you and so you will create new friends who see what you see, or at least accept your level of thinking. When you become free of those who wish to hold you back, you will not struggle quite so much to get *up*. This is what we are doing. We are going up out of matter. Spirit is rising and God is ascending.

Now; when you begin this process you will begin to see how you do not know all the answers. You, however, may begin to spout off like you have all the right answers simply because you are releasing the old and becoming the new. As you *become,* you will feel at a loss to *know* who you are. After all, for years you have operated from a certain set of values and rules and beliefs. Now that you are learning to change your view point, you are also losing or giving up your identity. Now, how can you possibly know who you are without testing your new beliefs to see how they fit? You will begin to feel and experience from a new level of experience and feeling. You are literally recreating you without leaving this material plane.

You have come to a point in your evolution where you will experience more than one identity in each life. You will no longer feel the need to die and be born again as a new identity. You are recreating you and taking on a new identity while still in the same body. Quite a new experience for you isn't it? God being born right here on earth. Spirit comes in and *transforms* life in the material world.

So, this is how you become God and this is how you begin to know your own God-self. Love you, allow you to do whatever is necessary to change, and don't hold back if someone you love is afraid for you. You must take full responsibility for moving into the light. It is *your* choice and *your* gift. I wish you well as you begin this voyage of discovery. Welcome to God's ninth book in this "Loving Light" series. Sit back, put your feet up, and let's get to it....

❧

*I*t has been such a long time since you knew God. You no longer trust God as you have not seen God. It takes a great deal of trust to allow someone into you when that someone is invisible. You are on your path now, you will learn to deal with new ways of learning and new ways of seeing all. It is not so difficult as you believe. Ascension is not so far away. You do not lift off into outer space. You simply tune-in to a new world that is ready and in place.

This new world has been in place since time began. You are not capable of seeing it at this time because you do not *feel* it. You will learn to *feel* it by learning to let go of *fixed* emotions. Emotions of pain and suffering must leave and so must belief in pain and suffering. This means that all revenge and resentment also must go. Wanting and waiting for someone to get their just punishment, to fit whatever pain you *believe* has been inflicted and deserves just punishment, will end. You will no longer desire to *punish* one another and you will no longer *desire* to hurt your own self for past sins. Your *only* desire will be to know God.

This is how we ascend. Ascension is desire used to know you. You begin to desire you in order to know you. And who are you? You got it! You are the big guy himself!

You are God almighty and you decided to reverse and not be God for awhile only because you are God and you have the ability *to be or not to be.* So, God is now reversing and coming back into himself. I know how this may not make sense to you now, but as you gain momentum on your return to God, you will gather greater ability to comprehend. For now I try to give you what you have the ability to receive, without pushing you into your fear.

You are so afraid of God that it is most difficult to get you to accept. You are so busy pointing at all the bad and ugliness, that I can't get you to focus on the beauty of this entire plan. Judgment must leave. There is no room for judgment. It does not fit into the energy that contains peace and harmony. Peace and harmony will come when all judgment ends. Now, isn't that easy? Stop judging and heaven is yours.

*I*t has been so very long since you left God and I wish you to return. You have not been in contact with God and you have not missed me, because you do not *remember* how it is to know me. I want you to begin to remember, to begin to see me in all that you do, and to begin to love or *be* God once again. God's desire is that you return. Your desire must be to return in order for this reunion to exist.

We are creating the merging together of God on high (or within) and God in matter (or below). You will know God when you see and *feel* him. He is you and you are him. A much higher frequency must be reached in order to *rise* to the level of thinking where God is.

God is thought and you are thought. You are the thought that created the stars and this universe. *Your* thought did all this. You have the power and the ability to reconnect God to God. You are the extension cord that is needed to plug into the source and *turn* on the light. You must turn around your thought. Thought must now be released in a new direction. No more *thinking* how bad it is to be bad. No more judgment.

From now on it is *all* good. If someone is shot I wish you to *think* high. Think, "Oh, boy he got to go back to God in his own way." Do not think how vengeful the one who pulled the trigger was. It is no more important than two children in a sandbox with squirt guns. No one dies! Get this straight in your thinking and it will help you forget about vengeful ideas. I want you to only carry *love* ideas. Loving is accepting. Love God enough to allow him to create his movie or dream in his own way. Do not block your own creativity by judging it. *Allow* everyone and everything to die or to be born. It is not wrong to die. It is not wrong to live. It just does not *matter*.

It's like going to a costume ball or not going, or leaving once you arrive. Some people leave because they don't *enjoy* long parties. Others leave because they don't want to be at this particular party, and still others leave because it's just time to move on! It does not matter how a soul or spirit chooses to leave the material world. He/she may stay or go at will. He/she may die at the hands of another, or he/she may take his or her own life. To take a life is to take off a suit. It is no longer wearable, or it just doesn't suit you to be in it any longer.

Sometimes a suit may be rather uncomfortable and so you may wish to *remove* it; take it off so you are not so confined. It is no different for spirit to take off the body so he might soar. The body keeps him *down*. It's like deep sea diving and wearing a giant weigh belt. It won't weigh you down forever, but for now it does. Don't judge those who leave this plane and move to a new level. It is no more than a child growing up and moving out on his own. You will not be able to *control* this child forever, so let the child go to find a life of his own.

You will find that you do not fear death so much once you *learn* what it is. Right now, to hear someone died is awful to you because judgment about death is great – only because you don't *know* where you go or what becomes of you. Then, to compound this, you have thousands of years of teachings *in* you that tell you of a place called hell or Hades. *You made this up!* Hades exists only in your minds. Change your mind! See it differently. You fear punishment, so now you fear death, as *you* on earth *use* death as a form of punishment. The truth is that the one you kill actually may have a much *better* time of it on the other side of this creation. Did you ever stop to think that where you are now, in pain and sorrow and revenge, may not be such a perfect place? Maybe where you go after here is peaceful, loving and free. *Think* about it! That's all I ask – just begin to *think* differently and you may begin to *see* a great deal more than you now see. You are like a blind man in the darkness and I am trying to lead you home to the light.

This writing is done from love. It is not meant to frighten you, it *is* meant to show you how you do not have all the answers and how you will someday *know* the *truth*.

⚜

Now is a good time to remind you to start at Book One. This set of books has been received in an order that is compatible with your unconscious beliefs. You are each fighting becoming God and to *stretch* you too far too soon will turn you off and you will no longer *desire* to *become* God. So, it is best to allow this information to be received by you in a formative manner. You can only receive what you are able to receive and this information has been channeled in a subtle direction in order to wake you *up*. I don't wish to frighten you and I don't wish to lose you. So please do your subconscious self a great service by beginning at the beginning. Book One is the introductory book and you will move on smoothly from there. The title of Book One is *God Spoke through Me to Tell You to Speak to Him.*

Now, when you begin to learn and *open* to the truth, you will find that you are not always happy telling the truth. Lies are quite important in your lives and pretending to be what you are not has become everyone's favorite past time. You all hate being you so much that you put on airs. You try to show to everyone how you are "better than," and in actuality you are better than *you* believe you are. But in most cases you are *denying* who you are and asking your friends to accept that this pretense is actually your true self. Stop pretending to not be this or that. In pretending that you are not so disgusting you are sending you a signal that you truly believe yourself to be disgusting.

If you get upset when someone repeats what you have confided in them, it is due to your own belief that you are awful and how could they say such an awful thing, or let others know your true ways. They may not be lying, but to you it does not matter, because the *truth* is the last thing that you wanted to leak out. You are all *hiding*. Stop hiding from who you are. You are not so awful. You will begin to heal by saying who you are. Be you. Show your true colors. You pretend to be what society expects and then you enter relationships and cannot understand why they do not last. It is because you *lied*. You presented an image of you that was not true. You showed the someone who you want to be, not the someone you are. You gave a false impression. People get upset with you because you tricked them and so they leave. They do not wish to be lied to, so they move on to where they can be honest and see an honest relationship develop.

Now; I am not saying to unload on every new friend or lover you meet. I am saying stay honest. Don't cop out by denying who you are; even if you see yourself as disgusting they may not. Why? Because you are all the same, so in believing that you live your life in a mundane or awfully boring way, you are convincing you that others are much better and others do not do normal disgusting things like you do. Talk about who you really are when you go out. Don't tell them how big or special you are. Tell them how small and insignificant you can be and you will truly begin to see how you are all one.

You do not need to brag, but it is okay to say you are love and striving for Godhood also. You will learn to know you by not denying you. Let you be who you are. Take off your mask and stop trying to be someone else in order to please people. You only wear this mask because you can't stand being you.

◈

I will now wish to discuss being raped. It is not wrong. No one ever does wrong. You will find this subject *most* difficult to deal with and that is why I selected it for today's class. You do not die from rape and even if you did, to die is not bad. So now I have you really upset. Rape is so very, very awful in your eyes and we must take the judgment out of you.

You are now in a position to see *all* differently. The reason you are in a position to see all differently is because you have been a student of non *judgment* since you read our first book, *God Spoke through Me to Tell You to Speak to Him*. If you did not begin at the beginning do so. Stop at this writing and begin in the first grade class on this subject of ascended *thought*. You will not help you to see how you keep yourself *down* in dense energy if you shock yourself with a truth that you are not capable of receiving.

Now; for those of you who are ready, I will continue. To have sex with another is to play or experience energy movement within the body. In order to have sex you usually use two people. This game can be played with one who wishes to simulate his or her own body, but the majority of you prefer two. So, to dance is stimulating. To touch hands can be stimulating and to have intercourse can be stimulating. In certain cases you are just not in the mood or frame of *mind*, so you lose the stimulation part of sex, or touch, or dance. When you are not in the mood your body is probably exhausted, or better put, the mind that *controls* the body wants no more input or stimulus. So, your mind shuts down to the *idea* of sex being fun or dancing being fun or touch being fun.

Now, all of a sudden, something that is judged as being good becomes something undesirable. How does this happen? How can you be in your best time ever one moment and the next moment you no longer appreciate the stimulation? It is all in your physical as well as mental makeup. In some cases you can build sexual tension to the point that someone simply touching your arm creates excitement. So, is sex *touching* someone's arm, or is sex kissing, or is sex actual intercourse?

Is dancing and gyrating to music sex? Is that why some of you get upset with new dancing techniques? Are body movements, that *remind* you of having sexual intercourse, the actual sexual stimulation? Is dancing sex? Is dancing with someone, without their consent, having sex with them without their consent? Is it their non consent to this act that is most dangerous, or is it the actual *act* that is so dangerous? If it is the act of dancing and not the forcing of yourself upon another, you should be aware that you do not know what is good for you, so how can you judge this or any situation as bad?

Where does sex begin and end? Who is at risk when *you* get excited over being touched? Is he or she, who stimulates you, in charge of what is occurring in your own physical body, or are you in charge of your own reactions to his or her touch? How can you begin to let go of judgment when you *see* sex as such a big deal? Let it go. It is touch. It is no more.

You freak out and carry pain for years and you suffer from sexual assault and rape and childhood abuse, and it is the violation of the rules that hurts you so. You are taught to not *touch* your own body and that it is offensive to you, and you do not even *know* that you feel offended by your own physical form. You cover it up and you get upset if you look upon another's physical form. You even lock people up for shocking you by exposing their bodies in public. *You, my dear sweet children, hate your own body.* You do not wish to show others your body because you have great belief that it is *undesirable*. You find you undesirable. How will I ever get you to love all if you can't even allow the body you live in to be good? You are so deep in your pain of judgment of good and bad that you punish you and everyone else for their sins. You are not *bad*. You are not ugly and you do not sin… not ever! Stop judgment. Give it a rest. Let it be.

I want those of you who are capable to let rape be. Let rape be no more powerful than one person forcing another person to the ground in order to lay on them and stimulate them. I have discussed in this class before how it is not advisable to override the will of another. You override and undermine others at work, at play and generally you control others a good deal of your life. This is no different and I wish you to give it no more power. To not abide by someone else's wishes is a common occurrence in your world.

Now; I do not wish you to go off half cocked and suggest that God has no sense of love and peace. I am love and peace, and I am trying to teach you to lose your pain of judgment so that you too may find your love center. I have written *through* Liane for five years now and I *know* her pain, as I am her and she is me. Her pain and suffering from sexual abuse in childhood is very, very dear to me for it has become my own pain. God is what you are. She is me. I am her. You are you. You are her. You are me. We are one.

What *you* choose to own *becomes* us. We are all in pain and due to release all suffering. We will learn to release our pain by letting it go and *allowing* ourselves to no longer use rules that create judgment.

Now; when you begin to break all the rules, you will create some confusion because you have been programmed for years and your body and mind are convinced that evil exists. It does not. Evil is simply blocked energy and the devil is simply fear. No big deal. Sex is movement, and violation has offended and disgusted you. Please be love. Love you enough to not *hold* disgust for your attacker because *you* will be the one who *carries* this dense energy. What you believe is what you get to carry, and it will eventually allow you to sink down with it. You no longer wish to carry dead weight or you would not be reading these books. You are on a very powerful journey *into* the center of God. God does not see through the eyes of judgment. God does see light. God is love. You too are light and love if you will just switch over to the light way.

I wish to thank Liane for allowing herself to channel this most controversial and heavy writing. It is not easy being God's pen. It will be rewarded.

*I*t is also good to know that you do not die. You

rise up out of body and move on. Some of you have experienced what you call death. You have crashed in a car, or fallen off a building, or just suffered a drowning; only you did not stay dead. A voice would tell you to go back or the doctors worked on the body you had left and revived it. This is called Near Death Experience and it is true. You do not quit existing just because the body stops.

Now, when you begin to die you take on a new level of seeing and hearing. You are so close to death that you may begin to lose touch with body. When you lose touch with body you experience without the five senses. You may feel like you are seeing and touching but it is all thought and belief at work. Only *through* the body may you truly feel touch. However, if you have a powerful dream you may remember the sensation of touch from your dream. Sometimes you are touched by others or even held down and killed in a dream. This will feel real; however, you know it is a movie being presented to you while you are asleep.

Most of you do not realize that while you are asleep you are at work or play in other realms. You leave your body and go to your destination and talk and enjoy another type of life. This is also how you die. You simply go to other places and talk and play and enjoy yourself until you are ready to come back as a baby. We are going to end this cycle by showing you how death is not bad or hurtful. When you no longer *fear* death, you will no longer be drawn to it. You fear dying, and it frightens you to lose a loved one, so death now has a big *hold* on you. You actually fear leaving body so much that you create death. Stop fearing death and it will have no *power* over you. You will go or not go, no big deal. It will be no different than going to the store. If you feel like going you go. If not, you don't go. Nothing lost, nothing gained. You may wish to go and return. This may become very fashionable in the near future.

No one is ever left behind when you die. This is a falsification tied to the belief that certain of you *belong* or are genetically attached to certain others. You are no more attached to one than to another. You are all cells in one giant body and you all belong to that same body. So, when you die (as you call it) you do not leave those who love you behind, because you do not go anywhere. You are still here and so are they. It is no more powerful than you being in your home and your family being in a different home. They are all living and playing and you too are living and playing. The communication between you does not need to end. You, however, will discover that you no longer have a lot in common with those who leave the material plane as their concerns for living in this world of illusion are no longer relevant.

Most of you will find it quite easy to die. You, however, find it very difficult to go on living. You are so afraid of your turn to die that you exist in a safety net that often strangles you. Fear of crashing and fear of being shot or stabbed seem to top your list of concerns. In actuality you seem much less afraid of natural disaster like earthquakes and storms. You mostly fear big crashes that are glorified by your reporters and it seems that blood is quite frightening to you. All of this will change. You will get no more upset over a gory plane crash than you will over a bicycle crashing into a tree. Hurt is hurt and trauma is on its way out. You are going to learn to accept life and no longer fear living. And you will learn that to be safe is no more important than taking a nap. Yes, it feels good, but it's not that big of a deal.

So, for now I want you to simply *know* that you will de-power this giant fear you have, and later we can actually discuss it without you being uncomfortable. Know that I love you and know that you will learn to love you enough to *accept* the truth about living on earth.

❧

Now is a good time to begin to discuss sex. So far you are very confused regarding sex and its place in your lives. Sex is in big trouble right now. You *use* sex to gain and you *use* sex to keep your mate and you even use sex to get what you think is pleasure.

So far most of you are afraid of sex. You are afraid to have it and afraid to lose it. You make excuses to get rid of it and you make up reasons to keep it. It is no big deal. It, as most activities on planet earth, has very little to do with anything of importance.

You are so afraid of sex that you fear connection or getting involved with another. You often have no problem losing a relationship if you have not had sexual relations with your partner. If you had sex everything seems to be different. All of a sudden you own him or her just because you gave your sexual enjoyment to him or her. Sex has nothing to do with love and it is a function that operates well enough with or without commitment. You, however, are so afraid of commitment that you use sex as an excuse to reel in your catch. Now you feel you have a good excuse to form control issues and receive a much needed commitment, before you lose him or her. After all, you all know how you love to own one another, and this is not how it was meant to be.

So, how was it meant to be? God was meant to enter matter and be *free*. God was never meant to be trapped in relationships or life. Rules are made because you are afraid of the *risk* involved in any given situation; "Oh, I fear this so I will make it more my way by making a rule that will make it easier to get it my way." You do not *need* to catch one another as you would a fish on a hook. Once you catch him or her you do not *need* to train him or her to do it your way.

You are so afraid of freedom of expression that you are stifling anyone who expresses differently than you. Now, one of the basics that I have taught you in this class is to accept. How in the world can you learn to accept when you are so busy changing everyone to make them acceptable? Of course, once you have made them acceptable to you, they may move to the next person who will then teach them how wrong they are to be like you. I wish you to learn to share without control. If you can not then you must allow each individual to move to his or her right place. You have made such a big thing out of someone committing to you and this is nonsense. I will now give you a rule to live by (since you are so fond of rules). If it feels good, stay. If it doesn't, you may leave. There, that's pretty simple and I think you will get it.

Now; for those of you who have children I wish you to remember respect. The soul for whom you gave your body to enter earth is not in a position to fight back. He is tiny and vulnerable his first few years, and after he develops personality he begins to act and react. Respect him and he will know respect. If you are already in trouble with your child, as many are, I wish you to remember "to respect begins with you." Respect yourself enough to give yourself freedom – freedom from anyone and anything. Commitment to a child is good if this is what makes you feel good. If it does not, you have other options.

Now, when you begin to commit your life away, be it to marriage or children, you are no longer in you; you have fragmented into those you chose to commit to. You will wish to discover who you are before you fragment further. Most of you are so fragmented that it will take some time to get you back *into* you. You are giving out pieces of you all the time. At some point in your future you will no longer feel the need to fragment. You have plenty of people now and it is no longer *necessary* to multiply and fill the earth. It has been done!

You will one day learn to simply love and float within creation. Nothing will be a strain, and nothing will be dangerous, and nothing will be important. You have lived your lives with a set of rules that were good because they got you to this point. It is as though you *needed* big protective boots to get you through the thick of it, and now you are ready to take off these big cumbersome boots that once protected you. Why? Because you are nearing the green grass of heaven, and to trod all over God's newly planted lawn in your big work boots would be a shame.

Please, take off your boots and run barefoot from now on. Everything has its time and place, but everything also moves. Change is very good. Change is coming for those who have asked. Did you know that you will no longer feel the *need* to procreate in the new world? Why? Because you will no longer feel the need to be connected to a body through birth. You will *know* that you are connected to everybody. You will no longer feel the *need* to leave an heir behind so a part of you will still be on earth. You will come and go at will, so such fragmentation will simply be silly. Splitting your energy to create more of you will become very out dated, because you will know that you are already whole and complete. You do not need a child to make you whole and complete, and you will never find a mate who can make you whole and complete. You are whole and you don't know it. When you do, you will no longer try to fill up your life with another's energy. You will realize how you are a total and complete God.

So; sex is just good fun and it was never more. You got afraid of not having enough, so you made sex the villain and now sex has a very bad reputation. Your sex is not creating AIDS. Your judgments *against* sex have created all sexually transmitted disease. Your vocabulary in discussing AIDS shows how you feel. You receive AIDS through blood transfusion and needles and sexual intercourse. You teach to sterilize your needles and wear gloves because it would be silly to teach that needles kill. How do you expect the new generation to feel free when you teach that sex kills? Sex does not harm anyone, ever.

Now is a very good time to explain how you are God. You are each God. No one on earth is 'not' God. Now, doesn't that make you feel better? You are not so bad as you thought. Look at those who you see as undesirable and *accept* them as God, as they are.

So, now we have you all upset because you want to get rid of your gang-slayer types and your murdering-plundering types. It is all God. You are all God. I will give you another twist on this. You fight to save the children and you put the children first. Who are the children? They grow into adults who are some of your hated ax murderers and rapists. One moment you fight to save them no matter what the cost and the next moment you fight to put them in jail or to execute them. A little out of balance, don't you think?

So, I no longer wish to see you put anyone's concerns before your own. You have all been taught to love others first and I wish to bring you back to loving you first. We are *all* God here, so no one comes before or after. You must learn that you are part of God. You deserve life and to recognize self-love. You will never learn to love the self by putting you at the end of your line of concerns. Want what is best for you and you will be loving and nurturing your own God-self. You are not bad to think of you first. You have all been taught to hate those who think of themselves first. I wish you to know that if you all began to think of your own happiness first you would all be happy.

The problem is that you believe you are in control of the happiness of others. You are not. As long as you believe that your happiness begins and ends with others, you will never be your own happiness. You are giving your "power to create your own happiness" away. You give it to anyone you blame for any harm you believe you receive. If you expect others to control your happiness, you then must wait for them to deliver happiness, or what you *believe* will make you happy. Why not control your own reality and get out of theirs. Yours is big enough to hold all, as you are all. You need not wait for them to say, "It is okay, you now deserve." You may give to you. Don't wait for them to give to you. Don't wait for a boss to treat you better. Quit, say, "I deserve better treatment." If your boss does not believe you do, he will not object to your leaving. However, he may realize you do deserve better treatment. Don't worry. You fear so much that you have created scarcity and lack. *Know* that you will always create better.

Now; you are body and ego so you don't yet *realize* your true identity as God. Maybe what is better for God is not what you might believe. Liane has let go of all her belongings save a few odds and ends and her clothes. She once *owned* lots of material possessions. Now she can fit all that she owns into one car. She has come a long way and this is progress. To the human ego eye (or perspective) this is not progress. I am freeing her rather quickly so she might be more flexible to do my work.

Now; money is a very tricky subject, because it means something different to each of you. What if… don't panic here, this is just a "what if" situation… what if money no longer meant anything? What if in the future your money markets and stock exchanges totally collapse from exhaustion, and an unrealistic view that you are dealing with anything but numbers, paper and plastic? Think about it. What are your paper, plastic and figures based on? Gold, silver? Who has in their *possession* gold or silver? Very, very few. You are playing a numbers game and when the game ends who will be rich? Those who know how to live and enjoy outside of the game, or those who are so caught up in this numbers game that they *fear* living without it?

Now; I do believe it is time to discuss food. You are all so afraid of life that you choose to strangle your body with food. You do not nourish yourselves; rather you purge yourselves of your feelings. To nurture is to enfold in health. I wish you to begin to love yourself with food and supply only what is necessary for your body to function.

You do not need to stuff your body in order to shut off emotional pain. Allow your body to express emotions. You are not afraid of knowing who you are, so there is no need to shut the emotions off by stuffing yourself. Let your pain come to the surface. If it takes a lot of food to satisfy you, it is because you are *starved* for love and substituting food instead of love. Be nice to you. Think good thoughts about you. Don't try to forget how awful you were to do this or that. Instead, I would like you to look at memories you try to forget and ask yourself *why* you have judged yourself so harshly for what occurred. Then you may let it go, knowing it was actually good and it helped to get you here.

Each event that occurs in your life has its place. It did not occur for no good reason. You plan your moves as you would a well planned escape. You have planned how to return to God and de-densify matter in the process. So; whatever you choose to do in order to create a new level of thinking is okay. You are *all* God becoming God. It is okay to know who you are and it is okay to let go of judgment that you were a bad child or teenager or adult. You were not. You were simply struggling into a new suit of clothes, and sometimes putting on a tight suit can be difficult as well as awkward.

You are not bad people. Your only problem is how you chose to use rules to guide you. You do not need rules. You are *free* spirit. You fly, you create – you are God. How can God have rules? God simply is. God is not bound by the limitations of the material plane. Come out of the restriction of materialism. No one is ever wrong. This is the spirit of the Spirit. Wrong does not exist. You created the fall of man by creating right and wrong. Do not continue to judge. Judgment is very, very strong and soon it will bury you. Take your power back. Do not continue to sink into the quicksand and muck and mire. Judgment is your weight belt that ties you down to this material plane.

This is a good time to advise those who wish to rise above the third dimension that to do so is as easy as changing how you think. *Your* beliefs and thoughts created these worlds of matter. When you begin to change how you think and believe, you will create new worlds with much greater love and peace and joy.

You are not so blind that you cannot be taught to see. For those who wish to remain in the material realms, you may wish to know that they exist for you as long as you believe *in* them. When you no longer believe in them, they will change into whatever *you* choose to believe in.

Isn't that nice to know? You control everything just by how you choose to see it. Free will is very powerful. Do you know, really know, what you wish to believe? How do you know if you won't even acknowledge your past? Come out of that closet you have been hiding in and ask yourself why you judge you for certain events.

If you get upset when people know you too well, you are judging you. If you dislike everyone knowing your business, you are judging you. You hide what you cannot deal with and what you cannot deal with is your own insecure feeling that you are wrong, or bad, or awful. Stop hiding. You are not telling the truth about who you are. You are God and you do not tell yourself this truth. If you did, you would no longer be afraid.

You are so very proud of who you want to be that you never give who you *are* a chance. You have this image and you want to present this image to the world, but your true thoughts and knowledge that you are just plain, old, disgusting, boring you, keep telling you what a farce you are to pretend to be more or better. Why do you pretend to be more sophisticated or better if you do not believe that what you are is just not good enough? Maybe you do not like you as you are. You do not like being you, so you hide what you truly are and show the world the identity you hope they can accept. By doing this you are telling your subconscious self that you do not *deserve* to be accepted unless you become something different than what you are. How can you ever begin to truly love you if your true belief is that you do not deserve love? Think about it.

Now I wish to discuss this problem you have with your own body. You all pee, you all poop, you all fart, you all sneeze and you all burp. It's not disgusting! It's simply the body removing toxic waste and relieving itself. How can you be so ashamed to discuss what you do? You *all* do it, or did someone teach you that you were the only one with these odd habits. Let it be. Let your body function without judgment against it for doing its work. You are so afraid to be human that I may never get you beyond the body level of evolution. There is life beyond the physical plane you know? And if you learn to love your body and all parts of you, you can all go anywhere together. It doesn't really matter if you choose to travel in body or out of body. As long as you no longer fear your body you will be allowed to float free. You see, fear creates friction that creates a binding effect. What you fear is what you get to own, because what you fear is what you are stuck to. What you let go of is what you eventually see, as you are no longer bound to it, but *allow* yourself to float *through* it.

You are God, so do not fear being God. You are human, so do not fear being human. You will one day have the best of both worlds, and you will *know* love, and you will *know* peace, and it will have absolutely nothing to do with the rest of the world and what they may or may not choose for themselves. *Your* love, peace and joy will come from you and to you. It will depend only on you and no one will have the power to change what you have created, because you have created from love. Love is thought, as God is thought. Think it and it is yours. You will know love when you know you. You are God – God is love. When you create your world of love, you will have the ability to tune it in or tune it out. No one else can do your thinking for you unless you give them the power to. Do not give others the power to influence your thoughts unless you like the place they are leading to.

It has been a good ride, but now it is time to stop. You have been spinning and falling and now you will stop spinning and falling and just be. You must not take this wrong; however, I wish to show you how it is no longer necessary to go down any deeper *into* life on this plane.

You may begin to enter a level of consciousness that is not quite so deep and you may begin to see all from a level of ascended consciousness. Most of you do not need to be so dense in order to stay down. You have received enough light energy to rise to a new level, but this transition is not immediate. You sustain yourself enough to keep yourself level. Too great a fluctuation and you become unbalanced. You receive just enough light to let you know how it feels and then you are allowed to stay at this new level while your body adjusts to this new level of vibration. Just as you begin to level off, you will again feel a raise or shift in your mental and physical vibration. Your spirit is shifting into gear, you might say.

As you begin to know what you have forgotten, you will become very active in releasing what you thought was your truth. As you release what you once believed and take on your new truth, you may discover a slight *shift* in your personality. You may begin to teach others what you are learning or you may begin to hide what you know, as you are now believing a truth that is above the level of thinking that is currently acceptable.

So; now we have you feeling and believing that you are different. You are, but you aren't. So how do you know what is good to share with others and what is not? You will meet those who accept you but not what you believe. This is not the same as not accepting you as you are. Some of you have great difficulty accepting little things about one another. You do not wish to love, yet you do not wish to turn away. You will find that to accept does not have boundaries or limits. To accept is just that. I accept; I receive. So, if someone wishes to *receive* you into their life, they will not care what or how you see things. This is how you will *know* those who love you and those who only love part of you. Acceptance is not incomplete. Acceptance is not conditional. Acceptance just is.

Now, for those of you who find yourself unacceptable to many, I wish you to look at how you can first learn to accept yourself. If you are not acceptable to your own self, you will have great difficulty convincing others that you are okay for them to accept.

You are all so afraid of not being acceptable that

you change your techniques, you change how you look, you change your attitude, when the only thing you really need to change is your belief – your belief in your own ugliness. Most of you do not have a very high perspective when it comes to your own personal traits and talents and abilities. You judge you constantly as not as good as, or just not good period. I wish you to begin to see at least one way in which you excel; one area that you believe you have done a great job, and use that to grow. Use it to show you how you are special.

You write, you sing, you dance, you raise babies, you drive a car, you talk to friends, you watch T.V. There must be one thing that you do very well. Use this one thing and focus on how well you do it and allow it to be an asset. I don't care if it's being lazy that you do well. We all have different ways of expressing our emotions and feelings. If being lazy is yours then you have accomplished something. You are great at what you do and you *love* what you do. Do not change what you do. Only change how you see you and how you *judge* what you do. Stop judging you for being you. You are not *accepting* all parts of you, which translates to not *loving* all parts of you. Let you be. Stop picking on you. I love you just the way you are and you *are* acceptable to God and to heaven.

The only thing you need to enter heaven is to change how you view you. Let your love for you allow you to see God. You are God. God is in you as he is in all creation. How can you be so judgmental as to tell yourself you are not good enough to be God? When you *accept* your

Godhood, it will be yours. The only hang-up is you. You must begin to *know* who you are.

Let go of judgment by letting go of fear of being right or wrong. Stop trying to make right or wrong choices for yourself and simply choose. Free will allows for any choice to be the right and good choice. There is not a choice that could be wrong, it is impossible in God's creation. I have created this dream world and I have allowed you to dance into it for your own convenience and fun. It was not meant to be a penalty box for bad plays. It was simply a dream that was allowed to unfold without restriction. The freedom of this dream frightened you. You frightened you. Stop being afraid of who you are. I have trust and faith which means that you have trust and faith. You are not the bottom of the barrel as you believe. You are actually the top of creation and you are experimenting as you go.

You will wish to know that you do not necessarily begin to be afraid simply by being on earth. You became afraid long ago and fear has been magnetized to you ever since. We are now at a turning point in your history. You are about to dump fear. You are beginning to see love and soon, very soon, you will know your own truth.

I wish you to know that I do not judge you for not accepting all parts of you. You are so scattered in so many ways that it would be impossible to try to contact all parts even if you chose to. With my pen it has been a very long process. First she explored past lives and then she explored parallel realities and finally she was brought home to this life.

She does not require a great deal of insight into her past. It seems that she requires only enough information to allow her to realize how she got confused in her thought process. Now she is in her early childhood unraveling her beliefs regarding pain, pleasure and punishment. She has little left to see before she will move ahead. She is you. Each of you has developed your own set of rules according to your own desire for freedom. If your family raised you strictly and you were punished at an early age, you carry a belief that strictness creates good and punishment will lead to that good. You, of course, do not *realize* that you believe all this, so you go about your life wondering why you have pain, or why you feel pressured and un-free to be who you are.

Un-free and stressed-out comes from being strictly treated, and now of course you are strict with your own self because you wish to be good. And, in *your* world, good is defined as strict and painful. Now do you see how this works? Your beliefs create your current life. How do you change your current life? You change your emotional beliefs. You see, emotion is attached to each belief. So now you must switch how you judge a situation as good or bad, and you must also let go of the good/bad programming or belief.

As you go along, you will find that you do not wish to let go of your teachings from childhood as they are very strong and without them you will feel weak and vulnerable. After all, you use your beliefs as a set of rules which keeps you in line, so that you have control of yourself at all times. If you were to let go of your beliefs, you would not know who you are or how to react or respond. All of a sudden, your beliefs go out the window and you go out that window too. Why? Because you *are* what you believe. Now you have just thrown you out, and must now make a new you so you will know how to act.

With no rules you get a little wobbly. For instance, this you knows that you must never wear a blue tie with a black suit. It is a rule you have lived by for years, ever since you were teased for doing so. So now you are a new you with no rules and you do not have the safety or protection of your old rules. You knew that as long as you wore the black suit with a nice complimentary color you were safe from teasing. Now you lose your rule regarding that situation and you feel unsure and weak.

I tell you this because I want you to know that you may feel vulnerable as you grow by letting go. Do not fear. To be weak is not bad, as you have been taught. How many times have you changed for the better out of weakness? My pen got very sick, and out of her healing and weakness came these books. You too may reach the top by first hitting bottom. A classic symptom of healing for an alcoholic is when he is so bottomed out he must change. Do not fear being weak. You are *most* susceptible to change when you are weak. I can mold you like soft clay when you let go of your rigid ways.

⚜

*I*t has been a very long time since you have known who you are. You drive your car and watch your television and you are not you. You are an alien and you do not realize that you are. You came here to investigate and now you have become so adapted to this vibration that you no longer feel like a visitor. You believe you belong here and you believe you own this place. You do not. You came only to transform and you do not own. You are a visitor, just passing through. While you are here, you go unconscious and you forget. You forget so thoroughly that you have no identity with your true form. You are not the suit you wear. You wear a suit to protect you from the damp and to ward off energy. You flow so well in your natural state that without your suit you would not be separate. Everything would move through you and you would move through everything.

Now; when you begin to come out of your coma you will be able to identify with who you are. You may have contact from "out there" or you may simply begin to know that you are here on a mission. So, what is your mission here on earth? It is to bring love. You are sent by God and it is to raise this dimension to a level of light that will allow it to see heaven. Picture this: You have a sunken ship and it is covered with crusty old growth and is thousands of miles down under the ocean's surface. Your job is to raise this vessel into the light. How do you do this? You have your men don a suit that is weighted enough to "hold them down" and you send them out with enough air to last awhile. They dive in, you keep a few good men above sea level to watch over and monitor this venture. Some of your men have been under or "down there" for so long now that they are becoming accustomed to the darkness and their suit feels very much like their own body. They are acclimating to the deep dark waters and no longer wish to come up. Not that they believe coming up is bad, they simply don't remember where they came from or how they got down there.

So now, what do you do? I suggest sending information to let them know that there is more to life than walking around a crashed vessel at the bottom of the sea. How do you think you would handle this? Would you leave and let them stay, or would you continue to assist in the waking up and eventual raising of their bodies back to the surface?

Yes, there are aliens waiting and watching and no, you are not crazy to believe in them. The only problem with aliens is, number one: you are so far gone that you won't even begin to accept them as help or rescue, and number two: you are afraid of your own shadow, so how can anyone who has more progressive ideas than your own ever be of help?

These books are meant to help. This is my communication to those who are tired of living in the darkness of a crashed vessel. You are not so afraid of waking up as you are afraid of more pain and hurt. The fear under the sea is brought on by the *pressure* to survive. The pressure of the water pushing against you is great and you are fighting the current with each step that you take. Now I come along and tell you to "let go, don't fight the current, flow with it." You, of course, have been struggling ever since you went under, so you don't trust flowing.

I will tell you a secret. Flowing is safe. Flowing saves energy and flowing will get you *in* to a less deep place where rescue can be accomplished. If you "flow" far enough, you will flow right up on the soft sandy beach where I can welcome you home. Do not give up. I am not leaving you. We *are* going to save you from your predicament. It won't be long now, because you have already begun to flow or shift a little. You will know that to move and change is very, very good.

Now; when you become involved with voices I wish you to remember that you are an instrument. You have the ability to switch off, to turn on, to send out and to receive. When you are receiving you may pick up many signals and many voices. This is why so many church leaders will caution you against trick voices who are imitating God. It is all God as you are all God. There are as many voices as there are people and even non-people. Energy communicates with signals and signals can always be translated into sound. You do not need to fear voices. You will know who is God and who is of your own making. It will "feel" different and some part of you will perceive this subtle difference.

The reason you do not trust voices is that you do not trust you. You have been tricked and deceived in the past and you do not wish to be tricked again. Some of you even judge God as tricking you into this situation you are now in. I did not send you out without your first asking to go. You volunteered to go down, so now you are upset and blaming God for your predicament. I will not comment further on this, but I do wish you to know that your fear and judgment keep you from the light.

Now; when you begin to hear voices, know that it is simply those who wish to get in touch with you in order to help. My pen had many voices before I stepped in and said, "Okay, it's time for her to speak with me personally." Her soul had become very protective of her psyche, as he had been her major teacher. He disagreed with my timing but told her, as all good teachers would, that it was her choice as she had free will. She could speak with me or not speak with me. She had a great deal of fear concerning God punishing her for her sins, so it took her a day to think it over, with a sleepless night in between. Most of you will begin to hear voices at some point. It is all part of you communicating with you. Leave them alone or speak with them. The choice is yours, as you have free will. If your voice is tiny and feels like your own voice inside you, it is. Nurture it and let it grow. The more you listen and trust that little voice the bigger it will get.

I do wish you would begin to trust voices. It's not the work of the devil, you know? You are so superstitious! You all fear the boogie man and you have seen too many possession and demonic movies. A voice is just a voice. You may listen or not listen, it is your choice and it, as all on this planet, is not important. One thing alone is important. That one thing is love – to teach you to peel away your layers and let your light out. You are jars of love waiting to open and spill forth your contents. Sort of like giant bags full of air, used to fill the interior of the ship, to lighten its weight enough that it will float freely to the surface.

⁂

*I*t is never too late to know who you are. You have been taught to believe that you are a soul who came into a body. You are, but you are also God and alien and life and energy, and on most levels you do not even exist. You are so vast that it is impossible to sum you up in a book. You have *stretched* yourself to eternity and now you are about to look *back* at who you are. You were projected out and now you are beginning to return. You are *thought*. You are a single thought that took on many, many possibilities. You have been moving in one direction for so long that it may take a little time for you to stop. You must stop, and then shift gears in order to be a reversal of what you now are.

So far, you have little to no trouble expanding, for you have done nothing but expand. Now you get to recede. You get to *unwind*, un-teach yourself, unravel the lies, touch the truth and allow all the protective, defensive devices to fall away. You will once again come back in to the center of your beingness – back to center or back to God. You will wish to know that you do not do this in the blink of an eye. This process is oh so gradual and is felt in many areas at one time. This is healing.

The explosion blew everything outward and now all the pieces are floating and drifting back in. God is returning to God, whole and intact. No one will be left out because we all belong to God. You have a great deal to learn regarding God and denial. Most of you are in total denial of your Godhood. You may *accept* what I tell you as truth, but you are not yet able to accept the role of God as being the role that you yourself play. So for now, we will work on keeping you calm and slow enough to not spread yourself *out* further. We will bring you in – back to center.

How do we bring you in and back to center? We begin by teaching you to accept what is and allow everything to be. This will stop you from kicking and struggling to change what is not yours. When you have calmed down enough, it may even be possible to get you to stop hating how you look, act and feel. The biggest changes you try to make regard you. Your own body and identity are pushed and shoved on a daily basis. If you feel the need to change something, change your mind. The *only* change that is necessary is for you to change how you view life. Stop beating you up for being too fat and ugly. You are perfect.

No one ever said you must fit into a certain image but you. Give yourself a break by breaking out of your own limited view of yourself. Not everyone sees you as badly as you do. The only reason you get so defensive if someone teases you, is because you have created such an awful judgment against what you believe to be your own inadequacies and ugliness. You have seen and believed what you saw to be true. It is not. You base your truth on how you compare to others and that is about as ridiculous as your heart calling itself inadequate or ugly because it does not look like a kidney or function like a bone. The beauty of the body is that it works with differences. It is not all one part that reacts and looks identical. It is many parts, all different, all supportive of this difference. No one would judge a liver as more beautiful than a lung. Well, maybe you humans would. You are so fond of judging.

Now; when it comes time to let go of your pride, you will find that you don't need to protect. Your protection and defensive armor will fall away. When someone says "you are not in shape," you will simply look to see and then agree, because it just won't matter if you are or not. When someone says "your nose looks crooked," you will simply respond, "Oh really, I hadn't noticed," or, "Yes, I know." It will no longer be necessary to prove that you are lovable the way you are, so you will never be offended, not ever again. Now, doesn't that sound nice? No more worry about what anyone else says or thinks. Why? Because you will no longer be judging you, so how can anyone else possibly judge you? They are just a reflection of you and your beliefs. When you let go of *your* beliefs your reflections change.

⊱✦⊰

*I*t has been a good time up until now. You all had a very good ride on this thought wave and now you wish to return. You are no longer in a position of control and this is what frightens you most. You are so opposed to anything or anyone who might fool you that you often deny even your own true feelings out of defense. Opposition is on its way out. The type of opposition you now create will no longer exist in your future. Most of you are very concerned with those who oppose you. You fight them and you struggle to prove how you are right and they are wrong. In your future you will no longer care what they say, or do, or think. It will have nothing to do with you and will have *no* effect on you.

Now; when you can get your own consciousness to

this level, you will be *free* of thoughts of revenge. If you do not feel that you have the power to sit by while someone talks about you, you are mistaken. You do have this ability. It is not only you but *all* have this ability. You have all been taught to *fight* for your right to be free, when in actuality, this fighting creates greater binding. If you can learn to let go of any situation and know that it does not matter what your opponent does or says, you will truly be free.

The biggest problem in this arena is that the majority of you *enjoy* mud slinging and even a good fight. So; how do I get you from a fighting to a loving mentality? This of course is most difficult. You are so afraid of being the underdog and you *admire* he who comes in and kills off the bad guys. The only problem with your good guy/bad guy stories is that there are no bad guys.

We all have been put in a position of defense. It is not wrong to defend yourself, however it does get you more *involved* in each situation. I am trying to get you uninvolved. To be uninvolved is to be free of a situation or to have no involvement in it. You have heard the expression "it takes two to tango." Well it does. It also takes two to fight, two to sling mud and two to do war. It only takes one to walk away, turn your back or turn the other cheek. Jesus didn't necessarily mean stand there and take blows until you are black and blue. The meaning is to get out, turn and run. Why are you so judgmental about running? Get *out* of any situation that does not feel good. Your pride and ego are very misplaced. It is okay to run, and many times it is very *smart* to get out of there. Why in the world would you ever believe that to fight is brave and wonderful? Who taught you such nonsense? Who taught you that to run is cowardly and that the man who does not wish to kill for his beliefs is not worth his salt? Someone really got one over on you and you bought it!

And now you kill and fight and it is brave to do so. How can you teach such nonsense to your children? Teach your children to use their instincts. When it feels like it's time to run… run! You are so out of touch with who you really are. You are not a yes man, who dons a gun and uniform because you are told that now it's okay, you have permission to kill from the head guy. You are the head guy. Say no to killing and fighting. Not because it creates death which isn't real, but because it creates psychological damage in you. It creates guilt in you and it creates *pain* in you. Stop hurting you by not volunteering to be used as a war machine.

You win your medals and get your attention for one brief moment, but you are simply being a volunteer for killing – a hired killer who doesn't make much and gains little to no respect from those who tell you to go. Pride is a very strange thing, and pride and ego must come back into balance. To kill is not your natural state. You have allowed those with money and position to tell you what is morally right and morally wrong. They do not know right from wrong or they would not be preaching right and wrong.

Don't go fight with Tommy and Billy. If Tommy and Billy wish to fight, let them. Do not get involved. Back out! Say "no thank you" to war.

*I*t is now time to discuss how you create illness. Most of you are quite ill and do not know that you are. You have headaches and constipation and premenstrual syndrome and you believe you are normal – it's just what exists in today's world. It is not. You are sick. Your beliefs and judgments are killing you. If you take pills for any reason, you are not well.

So; how do we expect to condemn you to illness on just a simple headache? I will explain. The head only aches when there is poison in the body. The body sends a signal that the poison is affecting certain areas and the brain receives this message and turns on the pain to signal you, so you will know to stop. Stop what? Stop thinking thoughts that are not pleasant and loving toward you. You are killing your own body out of a need to punish yourself for your sins. Stop punishing you. Stop hurting yourself and allow yourself to be loved by you.

Now; when I first began to discuss pain, I wanted to show you how you do not know who you are. My pen is quite normal in that she felt great pain and trauma as a child, but she buried it and forgot it. Almost forty years later her memory begins to open and reveal her secret. She forgot in order to mentally survive. Abuse is sometimes so emotionally and physically painful that a small child will not remember in order to protect their own psyche. When the child begins to remember, it is usually after years of dysfunctional behavior, and possibly illness. Most of you consider drinking a few beers every night quite normal, but it is not. It is trying to numb your own inadequacies and pain. My pen was no different. She drank, did social drugs (her term for it) and lost all her lovers, usually by falling out of love with them. This was one way of never really having to get too close to a man, and of course her sexual abuse occurred with a man.

Now; as she got older her pain and guilt and self-loathing began to manifest as pain in the physical body. Her emotional body was overloaded with denial that anything had ever happened, and no signs of evidence pointed to this abuse. So, she is overloaded emotionally and the mind is so busy trying to hide what her child believed to be her own ugliness and dirtiness (I use child here to denote her own five year old emotional, mental, spiritual and energy body that is still with her) that she gets sick. Not just the flu, but various symptoms and illness and back problems from this deep dark secret she carries. It has, after forty years, become somewhat of a burden and is beginning to completely take over the body.

Judgment spreads in the body like a giant disease. It penetrates every pore, until sometimes your body reeks with the overflow of poisonous fear. This becomes body odor and is also a signal that something has gone wrong within the body. You fear you killing you. The body knows you are killing it with your thoughts and your body sends out signals to warn you. You have lost the will to understand your own body or even to know it. Delve into you and find out who you are. Take out your demons and set them free. The Devil is only fear. What are you afraid of enough to not look? Stop hiding behind medicine and surgery. This is not how it was meant to be. Let your body know that you wish to heal, by asking it to heal and show you who you are. Talk to your body. Where do you think your cellular memory lies? It is not out or up in the sky, it is *in* you. Everything is *in* you. You *are* God. You carry *all* information, past, present and future.

Give yourselves a break by forgiving yourself before you even get started. You didn't understand that you were just being God adventuring through matter. I wish you to tell your body before you go to sleep, that you love it for being God's house. Allow it to know that you are going to heal with its help. Allow it also to know that you no longer judge it for enjoying sex. This is a big one, as most of you carry judgment toward your body for sexual stimulation. When Liane was hypnotized and regressed to age five she said, "He's touching me and it felt good;" and then she blamed herself for everything that happened to her for the next seven years, simply because her body responded to stimulation.

First you will learn that it is not your fault. There can be no victim and no villain when you take away right and wrong. No one is to blame because nothing bad occurred. In this ninth grade class you all understand this.

So; after you let go of blaming you for letting it happen, you will begin to forgive you for taking part. It is not a sin to have sex with anyone at anytime. A child often does not know what is occurring. His or her body gets stimulated, so she or he reacts to this touch.

Now she has judged herself and punished herself all these years, because she thought she did wrong and was so busy blaming herself for what happened that she lost part of herself. She was often sick and had several minor surgeries and, oh yes, one big trauma when a window fell from the top of an apartment building and landed on her while she was sunbathing at her pool. This was a real turning point for her as it stopped her dead in her tracks and she saw several of her fears come to life.

You too will create whatever is best for you to *see* who you are. You all carry judgment, you all are hiding something. If you were not you would not be in body, you would be here with me.

✺

*I*t has been very difficult to explain to you how you operate and who you are. Your language is so out of touch with the truth of reality that you carry many words to re-enforce judgment. You must learn to de-power words.

You use words to hurt someone and to anger

someone and even to praise someone. What you must remember is that a word has no power on its own. It only takes on power if you give it power. If someone says, "You are awful and you don't deserve to live," you get upset. Let someone say that same phrase in a language you do not know and there is no pain, because *you* do not translate what is being said into pain. If someone says, "I hate you," to every single person on the street and you are number one hundred and fifty, you do not even flinch when he gets to you with his "I hate you." You know how it has *nothing* to do with you and how it has only to do with him. Words only hold meaning for you if you allow them to. It cannot hurt to swear or to use what you call bad words. Words are never bad. People's thoughts create pain surrounding descriptive words.

So, if someone says "duck," you know to stoop down as danger may be coming from above. It is no big deal to be a little afraid of words. You have been afraid of a lot of things on this planet. Usually, whatever you create you fear. This is a pattern with you. Your creative ability is unknown to you and so you appear to be afraid of your creator, when *you* are your creator.

Now, when you begin to create your new world by seeing all differently, you may be the only one seeing your new world as you do. Points of perspective vary according to where you stand in your judgment. You are all drawn to be whole and this is why you are believing and seeing differently. Soon you will know the difference between the illusion and the truth.

*I*t is not such a very hard road to travel. To find peace of mind is as easy as opening the peace door. You have all wished for peace at one time or another and I wish you to know that peace is at hand. You will soon conquer chaos and war by conquering your own hidden demons.

Most of you are possessed, or in ownership of one or two deep hurts. These are known as energy blocks. They own you in the same way that you own them. Energy blocks are used by you to control. You control this energy by holding it in and denying it. You hold your secrets because you are afraid no one will love you if your true identity be known. If you do not wish to discuss certain topics regarding your life it is because you are hiding something. You are trying to keep something all to yourself because you have judged it as best to keep hidden for whatever reasons. It is not best. It grows in you like a suppressed bomb that is ticking very, very slowly.

Most of you are aware of sexual secrets, but there are also killing secrets. Many war veterans are totally at the mercy of their hidden secrets. They risk their lives to fight for freedom, but they also hold a gun and shoot to kill. Whenever you shoot to kill you carry guilt. The first time is most difficult then it gets easier. You are not free of guilt judgments just because it gets easier. You more than likely will kill at such a rate as to believe you are okay with it. Another way of putting this is to say you may believe you are actually getting quite good at this killing. After all, you have created a sport out of shooting at moving targets.

So now you have killed many and you know that to kill is okay because you were told to do it by a government, but some part of you does not agree. Some part of you pushes all the teachings from childhood down deep so they don't interfere in this job you must do for your government.

Now the war is over and you return to law and order and something is wrong... you no longer fit in. Why? Because you have been told to kill or be killed and you believed it and now you have lost your set of values. It is not true that you did wrong, but all your programming from childhood tells you not to kill and your child-self is angry with you for breaking your own rules and killing and being good at it.

Now you must look at a whole new side of your own personality and see how you (who would never hurt a fly) now have the capability to kill. You did not know this about you so now you are confused and unsure of exactly who you are. You are so confused that you begin to experiment with other, unusual for you, behavior patterns. You may find you now have murderous thoughts or you may have little to no respect for life. This is due to the fact that you were told to do something that was against your own better judgment. Had you been told that you were not needed to fight this war and kill others, you would have been more than happy to not kill, because killing is not what you really wanted. You really wanted a big pat on the back for volunteering your service. You really wanted to grow into a man you could be proud of and we all know that soldiers bear arms and are respected.

So what went wrong? Why didn't you get all those wonderful pats on the back for the rest of your life? It is because you keep your killing a secret. You stifle you, because some part of you does not know how to deal with your own violent and abusive side. You are shutting down by shutting up and hiding your truth. It will become less and less confusing for you if you will learn to discuss your hurt and disillusionment. You are not alone. You are in pain and confusion regarding your own ugliness, as many of you are. You always judge what you do not understand, as ugly, or disgusting, or unacceptable. Let it all just be. It is nothing and it is not important. Learn to talk about your secrets so you can learn to accept you.

You will learn that there are many who will accept you as you are, without judgment against you. Of course, you are so busy judging you that it may not make much difference. Even if you spill your guts about all your terribleness you probably won't believe those who simply let it be. You will believe that they judge you silently because your *need* for judgment and punishment is great. But, at least I thought I would let you know that the more you can talk about your deep dark secrets, the less deep and dark they become, until they will have so little power that you will actually bore people with them. Just for today... smile. Tomorrow will be much better.

❧

Now I wish to tell you about life. Most of you do not believe in living, you believe in struggle. You were taught that life is struggle and you must fight to get what you want. What you are taught is what you believe and what you believe is what you create.

So; if you were told that you were not good enough you may believe that you are not good enough. This programming or teaching will come out somewhere in your life no matter how peaceful and harmonious you wish it to be. Most often it is not war but struggle that drains you and defies all your efforts to truly find peace. Peace is a very small commodity and it weighs nothing. Peace is attained through self-love. Self-love brings *balance* and balance brings peace. When you have reached a point of understanding, within your own psyche, you will have arrived at balance. You need only balance you to change your world and no longer see struggle. You will no longer fear, as fear and love will become one. When fear and love merge there is no drain, no pain, no complaint. Fear will merge with love, as soon as all judgment has left that convinced you that *you* were bad. Without judgment you will not know how to punish nor will you wish to punish.

Your belief in an eye for an eye has created great pain. Often when you seek to destroy, it is a *reflection* of how you believe you should be destroyed. It is best to let go of all revenge thoughts, as you are killing and punishing you each time you wish for someone to "get theirs," so to speak. Do not wish harm on yourself. It is just not necessary. You will know if you do because it will be shown to you in how you wish harm on others. Everything you see here is only a reflection to show you who you are. If you wish someone else to receive ill fate, in repayment for the wrong they have done, it does not come back and get you. It has already got you or you would not see it projected forth in your life. You cannot project what you do not carry.

So; look at what you think about others because it is a direct reflection of what you think of you. Now, you will wish to know that, in reflections, you will also see pain as pain leaves you, and judgment will become strong as judgment begins to leave you. This is actually a good sign that, when you are emptied of these energies, you will be refilled with light and love. So, know when you are clearing and cleaning out God's house. Drink lots of water to flush toxic energy, and wait for your house to be all fresh and emptied of all your little black holes of misunderstanding and ignorance. The truth is replacing the lie and love is taking over for fear.

࿊

*I*t is not only your time for coming home; it is your time for peace and love. You will find that as you clear your anger at others, your truth will be heard. That truth is that your anger has nothing to do with anyone but you. You see yourself as having good justification to get angry at those who do injustice to you, and those who step on your toes, and those who push at you, and even those who ignore you.

If you are angry or irritated with someone's behavior, it is your own. Your irritation at another is a reflection. Look at this reflection closely. How can you ease your own pain? Are you angry because someone said you are ugly? It is only when you *believe* in your own ugliness that you will feel upset. If you believe in your own beauty you will laugh. Anything that hurts your feelings is done by you, because you have already hurt you by putting this belief in place. If someone tells you he does not trust you and you are hurt or upset by it, it is your own mistrust of your own self. You do not trust you. Some part of you has betrayed you by not doing what you want or thought best. You judged that 'you' (be he child or past life) and you set yourself *against* that part of you.

You now draw situations into your life to show you who you are. If you do not like what occurs it is because you have great pain in that area. If you carry no pain *nothing* will ever bother you because you will be pain free. Free is where we are headed. So; how do we get pain free? First of all we ask to see our pain, or as my pen was taught, you ask to see love. Each evening before sleep you may wish to ask God to show you love. Love is under all that is part of you, because love is your true essence. So when you ask to see love, pain and darkness must move in order to bare love for you. You do not require a great deal of effort in this assignment.

Most of you are so close to your most painful memories that many are returning on their own. This is the time for awakening and remembering. So; continue to remember and continue to request to see love. You will hurt as pain leaves and you may get upset with those who remind you of your own painful thoughts, but remember that it is best to get your pain out. If it is *necessary* to scream and shout do so. If you must hit or strike out, use a punching bag or pillows to kick and slug. This is a natural *instinct* that has been suppressed. If you were mistreated as a child, you wanted (out of a natural urge) to strike back but were not allowed to. So now you hit quite easily and don't know why. Do you wonder why you beat your kids so readily, or maybe kick the neighbors dog when he trespasses? It's your reaction to your own pent up rage. You never were allowed to kick or scream back at the world as a child.

Things are changing now and children are talking back and even terrorizing adults. This is you. They are your own fragmented selves projecting violence and destruction.

Once you begin to see that they represent your own child-self, who never was allowed to strike out, you will see how societies and even civilizations create, wipe out, and recreate. For now I will just say, watch your youth if you wish to see how much hate you carry inside of you. It must be removed. It must not stay. It is killing you.

≫⦙≪

Now is a very good time for you to *know* that you are *all.* There is no one out there or up there who is going to interfere in who you are. You will make all of your own choices based on how you see you and who you wish to become. If you strive for God you become God. If you strive for man you become man. You have a free will choice here and there are no consequences to either. You are allowed to stay, you are allowed to go.

You may wish to know that many have requested to go. You have been sending out signals for some time, that you wish to return to God. This is not necessarily on a conscious level. But, for those who wish to return we have hope for you. This is in the form of information that will prepare you for all phases of your return. Mostly, you will wish to know that you may decide not to leave at any stage of the game. You have created a sort of hibernation phase here where you are becoming God, similar to a caterpillar becoming a beautiful butterfly. You will hibernate long enough to change your programmed thinking, then you will emerge as a multidimensional, spirited being. You are now and you just don't know that you are. Now you walk, then you will fly.

A butterfly is a very diverse personality. He has a very soft body yet he has the strength and ability to change. He is very flexible. Even as a caterpillar he has the flexibility to bend in all directions. Soon, you too will attain this type of flexibility. Then, and only then, will you be ready for molding. You will be as soft clay and the God light that rises within you to give you birth will be in the drivers seat. You will become the most magnificent creature in all of creation. You will literally be God *in* his own created matter. You will be God rising up to form heaven right here on earth.

As heaven *becomes* on earth, the earth begins to shift and move. It can only take on so much light before it too begins to rise to a new level of awareness. It is as though you are giving birth to God in matter. You are matter, as you become all that you create. You are now accepting God light, love, whatever you choose to call it; intelligence is also a good choice. You are *accepting* and in the acceptance comes the initial rise of conscious knowing. We will all rise up and we will all love, as we will know that what we are is love.

It takes no effort to love, you simply accept in place of denial. You simply remember instead of forget. You have forgotten a great deal since you left. You need only ask to remember and your memory will begin to return. It is all you forgetting; now it will become all you remembering. It's as though you have an entire life you forgot. You got amnesia and don't remember, so your old friends and loved ones now frighten you, because you feel we are strangers. I am not a stranger to you. You became through me. You start and you end with me. I am the entirety of you. You must wake up now so we can finish this work. Wake up... see the light and remember how we are one.

It is not such a long time ago that we were together in all that we did. I have lost you only because you went under. You drowned in matter and now you think because you are covered with mud that you are mud. It is time to come clean. It is time to wipe you off and hose you down and see how you have fared. You will know you the minute you *emerge*. You will remember because you know deep inside how you have gotten here. Stop trying to hide. You are God. You know it. I know it. We all know it.

❧

*M*ost of what you now accept as truth is what you decided would best enable yourself to submerge. All truth is subjective. All truth is meant to provide you with the best and easiest protection at the time you receive it.

Everything is taught for a reason and nothing will ever last forever except change.

You are not the truth you were two thousand years ago. "People do not fly," was a truth two thousand years ago. "The earth is flat," was a truth two thousand years ago. "People do not eat other people," was a truth two thousand years ago. "A man owns his wife," was a truth two thousand years ago. A woman's place was definitely in the home, and "no one must go off to school each day." These were all true! The truth changes as you grow. You no longer burn witches for having special ability or insight. You no longer follow the advice of voodoo chieftains and you no longer would believe that anyone landing down from the sky was a god.

You have changed and as you change your truth has changed. The truth was the truth when it was first spoken because it was believed. Now is the time to rise *above* old boring beliefs that instill fear. You know for a fact that you do not sail out into the ocean and fall off the edge as you once believed.

You still have many superstitions and fears concerning what you do not know. God is not as you see him. You are basing your truth concerning God on *old* beliefs and even superstitions because you have passed your teachings down. Get a grip on reality! The truth is that you do not die and simply end. The truth is that many others are here, but you just are not *yet* able to view them. The truth is that you are never alone. The truth is that you no longer believe "the earth is flat and you will hurt yourself if you go too far out there," so stop believing that you will hurt yourself if you go too far into the unknown. You will not. Voices are not Satan's work and demons are simply *your* own fears talking back at you, and demon worship is simply you worshiping your own fears.

Do not judge life so harshly. Let it all be. It's no big deal! Only when *you* create great fear and trauma do we then have a point of concern. Stop killing others for killing.

༄

So far it is good to know the truth. You have not been punished for knowing and you have not lost your sense of humor. It is most important that you do not find fault with one another. In finding fault with them you find more injustice, and in finding more injustice you find more right and wrong. Let them do it their way, whatever their way is.

It is so hard to show you how you are pushing at one another, without getting you all upset. You push to change others out of frustration that things are not going your way or the right way. Let one another be. Stop trying to stop yourself from growing and expanding. When someone disagrees with you or your way, let them. It's okay to be you and to see it your way. It is not that you don't want to keep your way; it's just that you want everyone to agree that your way was a good way.

As long as there is a belief in right and wrong, there will be a belief that one way is better or worse than another. When you decide to do something your way you have chosen it because it works for you, or because it keeps you safe, or because you feel it will get you what you want. When you are hurt about someone saying your way stinks, you are actually hurt because your way did not get you what you want. You wanted the safe way, but now you are being told it's a stupid way. This of course translates to attack for you, so you have now lost your safe way. Or maybe you want praise and acceptance, so you do things very well (in your mind) and then are hurt when another tells you how you did wrong. It is now no longer praise you receive, but criticism. Either way, you now have received the opposite reaction you intended when you decided that your way was the best way.

So; when you find yourself in these situations I wish you to *realize* why you are hurt and not blame them. You are hurt because what you originally thought was good and right turned out to be only what *you* thought was good and right. You didn't get the praise or acceptance that you wanted, so now you are hurt and blame them. They are you. They only reflect how you get hurt and upset for not getting what you want from your own self. All pain comes from within depending on how badly you wish to hurt you. Some never feel pain in exact situations where you do, because they do not choose to punish themselves at that moment.

Even in physical pain, the pain comes from self-punishment. You call it pain tolerance levels or higher or lower thresholds of pain. In actuality it is you punishing you for your sins, to whatever degree you believe suits your crime. I am asking you to stop punishment. Stop fighting and stop pain. It is not necessary.

You will begin to see that pain is an illusion created in the mind to control the body. Body does not wish to be abused, so body sends signals saying, "you broke something," or, "you cut me, now fix me." You lost the ability to listen to your body so now pain is your signal. At one time your body could simply speak to you, but you are so afraid of voices that you have shut down your telepathic abilities all together. You will free yourself of these fears and be communicating with you in the future. You have a lot to learn and you are just beginning. The baby chick is emerging from his egg and has a whole new world to discover.

❧

So far it is extremely good to know that you wish to wake up to you. You are so afraid of dying that you are afraid of taking chances. Most of you are so certain that you will punish yourself with death that you do not trust most of life. You fear living as much as you fear dying. It is not often that you choose death over life, only because you do not remember death. It is not bad. It does not hurt to die and it will not be the end of you. You will learn that to die is simply to enter a new form of being. To die is to enter a different dimension of unreality, and to die is simply to go from here to there. Do not fear going from here to there.

Now; when you begin to show signs of moving toward death, you may encounter those who have very great fear of the fact that you have chosen to die. They will not wish to be with you as you will mirror their own fear of death. This mirror is, of course, a two way reflection. They show you how you really feel about dying and you show them how they really feel about it.

So, once you begin to die, which by the way you all do, you will wish to know that dying is a lie. You don't really go anywhere new or odd, or different. You just take off the suit, which enables you to unlimit your experiences from this third dimensional, materialistic plane. You now float! You do remember floating and you will remember this too. You have begun to take on so much pain that you have forgotten how you may float. Even in this dimension you may learn to re-experience this sensation. You may wish to experiment with out of body work, as some have enjoyed. Death feels much like this. You feel yourself float *free* of the dense material form you have worn for so long. You then *extend* your own energy out beyond this form and where your energy goes you go.

This is death. This is how it works and it is the end

of nothing, except the form you were wearing. You may wish to know that death is not an unhappy event for those who have gone. So, for today I wish you to learn a new way of viewing death. When your news headlines exploit violence and death I wish you to be happy for those who are now floating in their own time and space. They have not the restrictions that you have. They no longer experience the emotional trauma of this plane. They are free floating in their own choice of directions. They did not end, they simply became *more* by becoming less.

Get off this belief wagon that death is awful. It is no more awful than life. Stop creating so much fear around death. *Allow* death to be good. Allow all in God's creation to be. There is a reason for life and there is a reason for death. Stop interfering. If someone wishes to jump off a building in the middle of the day, let them. If you ask someone if they really feel that they wish to leave here, and they respond "yes," let them go. They may know their own destiny *or* destination better than you.

Judgment of death must end. The more experience (conscious experience) you have with death the less you will fear it. You are creating big black holes around dying. Open to the light of wisdom. You do not like hearing that you do not have the intelligence to understand. I am communicating this information as best I can for your level of intelligence. As you may have surmised, you are not the most intelligent life force in this universe. You *will* open and grow and *become* all that you are meant to become.

❧

Now is a good time to let you know how grateful you are to be here. Most of you have spent a great deal of time remembering your own pain and now you wish to remember your love.

You have been in a most peculiar situation in that you have not been able to see beyond the veil of your own truth. The truth of your own reality is so limited that you are expected to remain in it for just a short period. Most of you do not require, nor do you seek, great wisdom. You simply wish to know who you are and how your particular life works. It is not that you do not wish to be enlightened; it is just that you can *hold* only so much before you must release what you already have. You have not the capacity to say what you think and do what you want. You have so much information that tells you to behave this way or that way.

Now I wish you to become you. I want you to begin to let go of programming that tells you how you must act and begin to follow your instincts. Your instincts once guided you quite well, and now is the time to return to basics. You are not so much out of control as you are out of touch with your own self. Often you are taught to obey and follow others. Now is a time for breaking away and only doing what is meant for you. You are so afraid of being wrong that you constantly choose to go against your own intuition. Most often you are allowed only brief moments of release and these come when you are pushed so far that you no longer wish to take on more pain. Pain comes from being restricted and not allowed to be who you are.

So far you are not allowed to be you a good deal of the time. You are so accustomed to being who you were programmed or trained to be by past experience. Now you will begin to become a new you with the freedom to express yourself. You will learn to speak from truth and you will learn to respond from instinct rather than training. I know that you judge this word instinct and I know that you believe yourselves to be above the animals who rely on their instinct. Maybe you would like to know that you are not like the animals in many ways. They are simple and they do not wish to evolve to a complex level.

If you wish to be more like this you too may choose to. It is easy to become whatever you wish and there are many ways of doing it. So far you are most comfortable with the form you have chosen. This form has served you well and you are most able to work from within its perimeters. You find yourself in a very tight body but you are easily fluctuated within its boundaries.

Most of you do not yet realize that you are working *within* a body and you are not aware of your full capability to drive this body. It is as though you are in a brand new car with lots of controls and gadgets and no driving manual. You must rely on others to teach you how to use this car. The others are your parents and those who raise you. Now, when they began to teach you about this new high tech car, they had no manual either. So now we have all these cars running around with no one who remembers how to operate all parts of them.

You have only just begun to see who you are and what you can do with this car. Jesus came to show you how you too might use your body. Give it a try. Take it out for a spin on the open road and do not be afraid to use all parts of you.

☙❦❧

Most often you wish to be surrounded by love. You wish to surround yourself with family and those who love you. This is an attempt to feel secure and loved. When your family does not surround you at holidays you feel left out and lonely and depressed. I wish you to know that you do not need others to love you to prove that you are deserving of love. When you begin to love you it will no longer be important to receive love from others. The reason you feel that you need love from family and friends is because you do not love and respect you. You must learn to love and respect you.

Stop punishing you for not being good enough, or smart enough, or pretty enough, or handsome enough. Let you be. You are perfect the way you are and when you can learn to *accept* you as you are, you will have learned to accept you as the home of God. You each carry God. You each know God. You each are God. You are in me. I am in you. How can you judge you? You are judging God. You are judging my choices for you. Stop judging God. Your judgment is killing me. You are killing me.

So; before you get upset when the family doesn't wish to get together and join you in a celebration, be it the holidays or your birthday, remember how you feel about you. Are you really upset because they didn't wish to join you, or are you upset at yourself for not loving you enough to make it okay whether they come to you, or whether they stay away? Your feeling of "boo-hoo, nobody loves me" is a very big reflection of "boo-hoo, you don't love you."

When you do begin to *accept*, you will be *embracing* your own true identity as well as your own true nature. You will no longer require nurturing from outside of yourself because you will now have your own nurturing self to love you. And you *are* love, so this love has no end. When you begin to see how well you take care of you, you will begin to know how powerful love is.

You are just now beginning to see the wonders of it all. You will begin to share as you have never shared before. Most of you will begin to rise so quickly, once you have released pain and judgment, that it will be most difficult to keep you down regardless of what is going on around you. You will be like a crazy person who is happy in the middle of a mine field with bombs exploding all around you. Nothing will frighten you as fear will be gone. Nothing will sadden you as you cannot 'not' love when you *are* love. No one's death will hurt you as you will *know* no one dies.

The second coming is a very good and wonderful time. You are simply learning to change your mind, and in changing your mind you are changing your world. As you *become* more and more of what you are, you will begin to feel changes in your attitude. Do not judge these changes. Some things are leaving you and you are experiencing pain and hurt and anger, others are coming in and you are experiencing feelings that are new and feel a little out of place. Judge nothing! Know that you are God "becoming" and know that you are not going to explode; you are simply switching to a fourth dimensional level of seeing.

The dimensions are all varied and different, and as you rise you will begin to *feel* different and not yourself. Let it go! It is simply this sensation of changing who you are and how you view through this particular form. Once you see how you can change, you will begin to feel more comfortable being this new higher you. It is a wonderful time for you and for all who join in ascension. Let the others stay, as they have no effect on your rise. You may choose to stay also. It is all free will and it is all your choice.

When you begin to change-up you will feel many sensations regarding nerves and irritation. Let this be part of your natural adjustment. It is sort of like an animal who *senses* a storm coming long before it comes. You are returning, and sensory input will be changing as you do.

This may affect your nervous system. Also, as the fear leaves, it too affects the nervous system.

So; as Liane would say, "Hang in there," we're on the last leg of our journey back to God. Peace will come. No one who wishes for peace will 'not' see peace. It is not possible to choose peace and not receive peace.

☙❧

So far it is not known exactly when you will wake up. Most of you are beginning now. Believe it or not, this is the second coming. You are each coming out of your cocoon and you are all going to arrive in heaven. *Understanding* is heaven. Lack of understanding is hell. When you get enough light running through you, you will switch from anger to peace. Peace comes from *understanding* each situation you face.

It works like this. You begin to see something as not good or harmful or even dangerous. These types of situations usually have to do with you losing something. This is only loss because you see it as loss. So; you have this situation where you must choose between anger and understanding. As your anger rises, your light will diminish it and dissolve it into understanding. All of a sudden, what you thought was a threatening situation now has the gift of understanding the whys and wherefores. So, you now see your opponent as simply one who is expressing pain. Even in a major disaster it is simply someone expressing and *releasing* pain.

Even the earth releases her pain. You will find that if you are caught in the midst of an earthquake or hurricane it is just earth releasing. She is not judging you or punishing you. She is releasing her pain. So, if someone takes a shot at you or even yells at you, *know* that he or she is just *releasing* their pain. As with the earth releasing, I do hope you take precaution and run for your health. It is okay to run and hide, be it from the earth's anger and pain, or be it from another's anger and pain. Don't stand there and take it. You may leave whenever you wish. To be abused is not your purpose. To *be* love is.

Stop trying to show how good and right you are by your endurance of pain. Run when you are being hit. Run when you are being shot at. Listen to your valuable instincts. Listen to your voice. Stay only when it feels good. Know what makes you tick. Stop pretending that once you begin something you must stay to the bitter end. Let it go. Leave whenever you feel like leaving. You are making yourselves prisoners of your lives and families and property. Know that you are you no matter where you go, so *you* won't change by running, but your situation certainly will. Give you a break by letting you listen to your own natural guidance. I know you all believe it is best to stay and fight or stick it out, but sometimes things happen to get you to move. It is that simple.

Begin to listen and you will begin to hear. Teach

yourself to let go of what is right or wrong and allow yourself free will choices. Stop following the rules. Stop following period. Be you. Express as you. Love you just as you are.

∾⁂∾

Now is a good time to begin to see how you do not wish to be one. You have many parts of you and you do not wish to connect with all of you out of a fear that you will be hurt or upset. Most of you are so unaccustomed to being you, that if you were to all of a sudden become your true identity you would not know how to deal with all the sudden changes in your perception. Therefore, this process is done slowly and gradually. You are waking up to an entirely new reality. One in which you will see, think and live differently than you now do.

You may begin to lose old friends and gain new understanding ones. You may divert from family interest and you may leave your family altogether. You are shifting consciousness, and in the true reality, no one person owns another. Being a parent is no more important than being a child. No one ever owns any part of another being. You are not to believe that you have a special hold on someone simply because you clothed them or fed them. *No one owns!* You are all children of God and some of you wished to *share* your home and food, and so you volunteered to invite others to be your children. Children owe nothing to anyone. No one owes for the right to live. Leave your children alone and they will do whatever they came here to do. Make them into miniature versions of you and they may have more trouble waking up than you. You must *allow* them to express their own creative insight. You were not allowed to and now you have the opportunity to see it differently.

You are not slave to your children. They do not own you. You are free to give them away if you do not feel the need or desire to raise them. There are many who want children. There are many who don't want the children they have. When you begin to get honest enough to share your true identity, you will get honest enough to say, "I don't want to raise children." You are not bad for not wanting to fragment yourself further. Eventually, fragmentation will end. You have been splitting and multiplying in this fashion for so long that it will take you awhile to learn that it is not necessary. Now is the time to become *one*. How do you become one when you are still sectioning off parts of you in an attempt to make you more? You become more by becoming less.

So far it is very difficult for you to grasp some of these concepts, but I will continue to tell you the truth until you begin to remember. Jesus even suggested to Mary that she was no more important than the others. This is truth. People do not own people no matter what rules you have decided are best to obey. Honor thy father and mother has harmed many a child. You do not deserve respect without showing respect. Don't expect to receive what you do not give.

Now; for those parents who have a "bad seed" on their hands, I wish you to know that the choice is yours. You are simply a caretaker of this child. If you choose to abandon this child you are not bad, you are simply getting rid of a problem child. I know that you have been taught to *solve* problems by changing them, but now is a time for changing you, not them.

It is difficult to teach this information, as you have great judgment *against* it. Let judgment go. When you can let go of judgment and simply make your choices, for yourself, based on your own intuitive ability, you will be not only respecting you, you will be honoring you. Learn to honor you. Learn to love you. Learn to put you ahead of them instead of putting everyone else's needs ahead of your own. Learn to let you be.

You are taught so powerfully to put everyone else ahead of you, that you *accept* that concept readily. But let me even suggest that you put you ahead of them and you think that suggestion is awful. This will give you just a hint as to how much you *dislike* you, and you don't even know it. So; how were you programmed to dislike you? How did you sink so low on your own list of priorities? You became last by being told you were last. You were taught as a child to trust adults, respect adults, speak to adults, run to adults for help and never talk back to adults. Who were adults? Everyone but you. So now you are a child in an adult body and you still carry these beliefs, so you let everyone else get the respect and honor. You even honor things above your own self. You were punished for breaking things, so now your little child mind has programmed you to believe that all those precious things are more important than you.

This must end. No one and no thing is more important than you. You are most important in your life. No one else can heal your life. No one else can fix you. No one else can allow God into you. No one else can love you, because you never give love away, you simply are love. This concept of getting and giving love is totally erroneous! You cannot give or receive love. *Love is*. Take a flashlight and try to pass that light to another flashlight. You cannot! You can see with your flashlight and even shine your flashlight on another to show them light. But the light shines from your flashlight and when you stop shining your light in their direction you still have your light. You gave nothing away and every individual has his or her own flashlight. Now it is time to turn-on! Wake up and know that you are God. Honor you, love you. Stop hating you and putting you last. It is not your proper place. You are all the first, the last, the beginning, the end, and absolutely everything in between.

❧

So far it is not your fault! You do not own wrongdoing. You are not wrong. You are not bad. You are love. You are light. So; any judgment that you carry against you for emitting bad behavior is simply not true. Begin to know that you do not judge you for love and punishment against yourself, but you do judge you for hatred and anger. Hatred is part of fear and fear is simply your bad judgment. Now, how can you make hatred out to be so awful? Hatred is not love, but in the *big* picture there is nothing but love. So let it go. Let all judgment go.

For now I wish you to know that you are all light! You got a little dusty and messed up while waiting around to be turned on. Do not judge yourself for the length of time it took to *arrive* in matter. It was a good trip in, and everything went as expected. Most of you do not wish to be bad guys, so stop judging yourself as bad guys. No one takes away from you and you never lose. Why is that? It is because you have nothing to lose. You do not *need* material possessions in order to exist, and you do not need money in order to exist, and you do not need jewels in order to exist. You are love. You are light. You will draw unto yourself your just rewards. When you are in need, your needs will be met in some way. It is not necessary to shoot someone for stealing your stuff.

If you do shoot someone for stealing your stuff, I do hope you remember to not *judge,* for this situation creates more trauma in you. I try to teach you the truth. The truth is that no one ever ends, but when you shoot someone you create greater judgment, which leads to greater guilt, which leads to greater punishment, which leads to greater pain. Why do you think religion preaches that you must be nice and kind and loving? It is not because God said so, it is because you are bringing down the density of this planet. You are running your energy backward. You are going down when we wish to rise up.

Leave well enough alone. Don't create greater fear by killing and don't create greater judgment by choosing right and wrong. Let you be and let them be. *Do not judge!* Can you do this one thing for me? Judge nothing that you see. I wish this to be your assignment for this week. Go out into your world and while you are in it I hope you remember that it is simply *your* world, with *your* truths, *your* beliefs, *your* concerns and *your* fears. So, go out into *your* world and let everyone else live according to their truths, their beliefs, their fears. Don't judge them. If you can learn to become aware of where you judge, you will learn how judgment works. This will be your assignment for this week.

If you have trouble in regards to letting the rest of God's children create and interact in the way they choose, I suggest you pretend they are God doing what God asked them to do. This will get you to realize that it is really none of your concern. Your job is to be you and their job is to be who they are; painter, housewife, slob, neat freak, repairman, lumberjack, hijacker, policeman, hooker, pimp, bartender, rapist, molester, bank robber, priest, televangelist, cab driver, doorman, teacher, prisoner. Leave them all alone. Do not judge any! Do you think you can do that? Just let my creation be. It is not for you to judge.

≈≫

I wish to tell you a secret. This secret is very, very big – "You do not know how to love because you have not yet *'become.'* As soon as you *'become,'* you will be love." You are still in the process of coming into life. You are on a journey into matter and this journey has taken some time. Now that you are at the door of giving birth to you, you are most impatient.

This is the celebration. This is the time you have all come here to enjoy. See everything around you as being part of this process. No one is off base. No one is wrong. Everyone is simply becoming. Now; when becoming begins to be speeded up, you will wish to rise up to meet your new self. As you rise you will begin to feel new sensations. This is you coming out of matter. You are being pulled out of matter in order to receive God. Yes, I know that you *are* God but you don't remember that you are. So, this is simply a process of God merging with man and man becoming God. To know it, is to believe it – and to believe it, is to create it in matter. Elsewhere it is known. It is only here that you do not know that God is you and you are God.

Now; when we begin this process of rising up you may not feel so well. It is as though you have always been drugged and now you are coming off your drug. This is rehabilitation time, and at first, your body will crave the old way of believing as it has always had its drug in order to ease the senses into matter. No drug will be allowed in God. You will not find it necessary to use this fictional way of believing now that you are coming out of the illusion. You are not to be afraid of coming off your drug. It may be uncomfortable as you withdraw, but you will be so much more by letting it all go. You will become the life that is meant for you. You will be *free* of fear and limitation. You will create from love. You will find your peace of mind and true happiness simply by looking at it.

You do not know how to see what is right in front of you, because you are on drugs and wearing blinders. When you are on drugs you see distortions and illusions. This is the drug of fear and limitation. This drug will leave as you move into the light. This drug is untrue reality. This drug is war and violence and pain and stress and anger. When you stop believing *in* these, they will dissolve along with the pain that belief in them creates.

So; how do you stop believing in what you *know* you see every day on your news and in your life? Translate it differently! If you see someone get very angry and yell, get out of their way and wonder what is making them so sick that they are vomiting up anger. They are simply sick from disease of the mind and emotional body. They are not bad, they are just vomiting up the bad stuff they swallowed; the beliefs that stifle and strangle and choke them. They are so sick from anger at life or at someone who once punished them, that they must regurgitate what is making them ill. It has nothing to do with you any more than your child vomiting has anything to do with you. See it all differently and *your* belief in violence and anger will change. When your beliefs change you change, because you are your beliefs. Your entire identity is created by your belief in who you are.

Now, for those of you who do not wish to see it differently, this too is okay. You have free will on this plane and if you desire to stick to this illusion you may. You may choose your destiny and you may choose your life style. It is all up to you. No one need take responsibility for another's choices and no one need wait for another to wake up. "There is always another bus," as they say. So, you know you can get to your destination whenever you are ready to catch your bus out (and up). So for now I will simply say "aloha" for today. This is Hawaiian for hello and goodbye – such a nice word.

∿

*I*t is not so often that you are flexible. Most often you have your own point of view that you wish to maintain. Not only do you wish to maintain your own point of view, you wish to make others *see* this same view point. Most of you are so afraid of being alone in what you see that you try to convince the others to join you. You are most accustomed to being together as a group and you need group support. You, of course, only believe that you need support. You actually only need one thing… you.

You will begin to know how to survive alone. It will no longer be necessary for everyone else to see as you see, or to understand your views. Once you begin to love you, you will find that it simply does not matter if others agree with you or not. It simply will not matter if they agree with your choices, or your view, or your beliefs. Nothing will matter. Nothing will be important because *in God* nothing has consequence. In God everything simply exists and "so what" if this occurs or that occurs. It's just not important.

So; when you begin to see God you will begin to not care. This will be one of your first clues that you are finding love. Loves does not care if you have approval. Love does not judge "not having what you desire" as bad or hurtful. Love says, "So what, I love me, I am love. There is nothing that can harm me in any way." When you can freely flow through life you *are* your own energy moving into creation. When you flow forward you take you with you. When you flow you move ahead and around, and as you move you spread and grow.

So; if you move "up," you take the rest of you "up" with you. When you move down you take the rest of you down with you. I wish you to know that movement down is not bad, it is simply not where you wish to be at this time. You *have* been there for some time, so don't "hang in there" if up is where you want to be. Don't continue to believe in right and wrong if you no longer wish the battle of these two energies. If you wish for peace, do not believe in polarities and lock out one in favor of the other. You are creating war by doing this. It is your own war that you create. It is a battle inside of you that causes you great pain.

Now; when you begin to rise up you will often lose your need for struggle, you will just "give up" and "give in." Struggle will simply be too much for you. This is good! You will wish to know that when you let go of struggle you begin to find peace. Struggle is fighting to *change* anything that occurs. Fighting is struggle. Let it all be. If a situation does not feel good avoid it. If it does feel good stay and learn what you want, but do not *struggle* to change others or to change situations. I know this is the exact opposite of what you have been taught, but you are rising up out of fear, and fighting, and control. Fighting and struggle were good to keep you *down,* but now you wish to go *up* and I am showing you how to. So; new rules for a new age of peace. These new rules are actually beliefs. I gave them to you in Book Three when I took away your Ten Commandments. These truths are: Be Love. Be Light. You are Love and Light.

So; there you have it. You are now on your way up! Let go of all that holds you down. These are your material weights. They keep you down *solid* in rock. They harden you and solidify parts of you. If you wish to be spirit and float free of dense matter, join the air patrol. We are rising rapidly and our training is very simple. Our technique is to learn to change our minds and our beliefs. This is all it takes to fly. You have been grounded only because you believe you have no wings. I am here to show you how to rise up. You requested it and I got a volunteer to let me come in. You are now reading a message from God, created by you and sent through one of you. Why? How? You requested help in this area and I gave you this free will choice by allowing you to contact me whenever you felt hurt.

Stop pretending you don't *know* who you are. You do know and you do want to return. Most of you know that you do. It is just this portion of you who is dead. You will wake soon. You will come alive! The unconsciousness is simply a very deep sleep to allow you to adjust to dense matter. It is safe to wake "up" now and begin to rise above matter. Come on, be with God. See the light. See the love. Now; when you first begin to wake up you will feel sluggish, just as you do when you are waking very early in the morning. You early risers will see the dawn of this new age and it will be beautiful! Most of you will wake a little and roll over and snuggle back in for more sleep. So please, those who are waking now, try to keep your enthusiasm down a little, so as not to disturb the others who still sleep. They may get crabby if you wake them before *their* wake up call.

*I*t is not too late to learn you have been taught fairy tales to get you by, and now I will teach you how to see the truth and know true peace. When you were first taught about right and wrong you had a great *need* to separate. It is done. You have separated and now you are returning to you. You will begin to return in remarkable ways. Some will see great change and others will see it a little at a time. It does not matter how *you* choose to see this new world of yours. You will not care what the others are doing, because when you come from love you have no attachments to how you see others. It is not important how they look or how they live their lives.

Most of what you have been taught has been to keep you *safe*. And why teach safety? Out of a *fear* of danger, of course. So fear has been your guide, your teacher, your leader. Let go of your belief in fear and begin to teach from love. Love sees no danger, love sees no pain; love sees no fear. Love is joy in all. Love is peace no matter what occurs. Love is happiness without fear of "not having." Love is heaven brought down to earth. The days of love are right around your corner, next door to heaven. You are learning now how to be uncovered or unraveled. Soon your cupboard will be bare. Your subconscious mind will give up what it believes to be true for you and you will begin to rise.

Your level of consciousness will begin to rise up to meet your new world. You will be able to live in total peace and harmony without going anywhere. You will *change* how you view your world and as *you* change what you believe you see, you will open to an entirely new vision. The trick is in the eyes. The eyes are colored by what is in the mind. When your mind is centered in peace, your eyes will see peace. You are your mind. You are what you believe. You begin to create a world by first imagining it. Then you begin to project yourself into it. Sort of like a dream you are seeing, and before you know it you are not only viewing this dream, you have projected *into* it. This is where you are. If I can get you to change your mind about what you see, I can get you to project *out* of one world and *into* another. Out of fear and into love. Out of hate and violence and confusion and into peace, love, joy, harmony. You will learn to get there by looking inside of you, by watching to see how you believe. If you have difficulty seeing your own beliefs, simply watch those around you. As I have said before, everyone in your life is a reflection of you.

Did you ever notice how you each see the same person from a different point of view? One of you may see him or her as intelligent, sophisticated and cunning. Your friend might meet this same person and only see him or her as nice, and kind of dumb. Who is right? You both are. You can *only* see in another, what you carry. If you believe yourself to be dumb you will see dumbness. If you believe yourself to be cunning and intelligent this is what you will see. The level of your own cunning and intelligence will be judged, by you, as you see those you are judging. If you see this person as very bright, intelligent and cunning, but the person next to her or him as not worthy of his or her position with this bright, cunning one, then this is you believing you have this level of cunning and intelligence, but you also don't believe your cunning and intelligence goes very far.

If you can learn to be very careful as you look in your mirrors, you will learn to see you and what you believe. When you look take *care* not to judge where you are or how you view you. You will begin to see you from an entirely new perspective. Don't try to change you, try to change your mind.

❧

*I*t has never been my intent to lead you out of this plane and into heaven. It has, however, been yours. You decided long ago that I would be here when necessary. It has been a very long time since you left and you do not remember how to tune-in to you. You are me. I am you. You will begin to see that all is actually connected. I am connected to you and you are connected to me. You are connected to this plane and you are connected to heaven. Heaven or paradise is a part of you just as I am. It is all *in* you. You simply tune-in and there it is. No more pain, no more struggle.

So, once you begin to see heaven you will actually

be seeing you. Some part of you not yet explored by this particular you. You will begin to know how you tick. You will begin to tune-in to more and more of you. You will begin to know who you are. You must enter you in order to know you. This is why I teach enema. Enema is a very easy and quick method of rediscovery. It literally triggers your cellular memory. It washes out toxins in order to "open you up." It is not unsafe. It is smart and practical and energizing. Enema will turn you on and turn you inward. It has the same effect as cleaning out a deep wound. As long as there is infection and goo in a wound it cannot heal. As long as there is toxic waste *in* you, you cannot heal.

So; learn to take good care of you by cleaning you out. If you do not wish to do enema, go to a colonic center for colonics. You must begin to heal before you can get *clear* undistorted messages from you to you. Think of you as a very fine piece of technical equipment that you must keep very clean and running smoothly. This equipment is priceless, so please remember that when you don't feel like keeping it clean.

Now; when you begin to clean out your toxic waste and to learn to ascend into level four and beyond, you will not need to pack a bag. You go nowhere and everything you see will be new to you. You will ascend into a new level of seeing life. Some of you will go even higher and see love in its purest form... God's love. You will know that you are doing this and you will know that it only takes one thing to ascend... you! Nothing else is needed, just you and the *will* to rise up; to ascend.

So, when you begin this journey within, know that you discover you alone. No one else will see what you see unless it is a joint effort in exploration. Sometimes permission is given for one of you to enter another, but this is rare at this time. Know that as you discover you, you will be unraveling you all the way back to your beginning. And where is your beginning? Were you an extraterrestrial? Were you an amoeba who sprouted limbs at one time? Were you simply a beam of light who zapped into the hemisphere and grew into a prototype? Did you evolve from an ape or did you evolve from your own awareness? Many of you will see many different adventures, so don't get too hung up on them. There are as many ways of entering your dimension as there are realities surrounding it. You could be one of many who injected into creation in one way or another.

So, when you begin to unravel, you will ultimately know who you are. When you begin this process I wish you to know that what you see is often what is known on some level of creation. If you do not agree with what you see it may belong to another. You do have the *ability* to determine what you created and what another projected out for you to believe. If you have problems in this area just let it go. It is not important how you got here and I do not wish you to dwell on it. Know you and allow you out of your subconscious. If what you see makes you uneasy, let it go. Don't judge it, just look at it and say, "Gee, I wonder how that got in me." You will see all as you unravel, so don't get too concerned about past lives, etc.

When you begin to see this life it will affect you strongly because you are still *in* this life. Any pain or suffering will seem greater than past life pain and suffering. This is only because you are *closer* to it and it has not had time to defuse and melt away. You will do well to let it out emotionally and get on with your healing. Take whatever time is necessary to confront your pain and be kind in your release. It is not so bad to express suppressed emotions as you believe. Crying is very good for this and hitting or kicking a pillow will help your body release its pent up anger regarding this pain. Know that you will find it difficult to be kind and loving and giving to others when you are clearing your own pain. Know that you will not die from it; you are simply clearing it out of your body. You will die from it if you leave it in. This is how you created this myth called death.

≈⫶≈

Now I would like to discuss your idea of a good time. You believe it is good fun to be excited and spin and evolve quickly. Most often you find it very easy to enjoy friction. As you begin to release pain, you will find that friction is no longer desirable. Excitement becomes something you can live without and you no longer enjoy being high.

Excitement is strong physical emotions caught up in your mind. When these emotions come into play you are excited or in a state of apprehension. As apprehension grows, you become nervous and full of fear. Why? Because the very thing that excites you actually frightens you. You are excited by fear. I wish you to know, that when you begin to feel excitement in regards to a planned trip or a new big purchase, it is simply your fear as to whether or not this adventure or venture will pan out.

Most of you do not realize fear when you are in it. It is not so much that you don't acknowledge it, but you simply don't recognize your own emotions. No one has ever taught you what your feelings are or what they mean. So; one person may translate one feeling to be good while you translate it to be bad. It has to do with association and what experiences you have been associated with when you were *feeling* your emotions.

Let your emotions be. Do not judge you for feeling fear. It is a good idea to go into your fear and really experience the emotion. If you begin to perspire or heat up recognize it. If you get butterflies or nausea, feel it, know it. Experience your emotions rather than trying to calm them or shut them off. They may be pent up emotions if you have always denied them and tried to calm them or turn them off. I wish you to learn to *feel.* Learn to know you and no longer suppress your feelings. Get them out. Let your body speak to you. You will be beginning a new relationship with you. Your body has been shut up, denied, rejected as offensive and told it does bad things. How can you possibly learn to love you when you not only don't trust your body, you don't understand its signals nor its intentions? Learn to love you by loving *all* parts of you. To start with the house you live in is very good.

❧

*T*here will come a time when you are most available for ascension. This time will be when you have released the beliefs that hold you down and keep you solid. You have many of these beliefs and they are all centered around judgment, which is basically right and wrong or good and bad. You will learn that you do not need to believe in bad to get good and you do not need to believe in wrong before you can have right. All things are good and right. Nothing is wrong or bad. Leave it to you to *depend* on these polarities for your security.

Now; as I begin to draw you out of the mud of your own convictions, you will be a little upset as you lose right and wrong. You have depended on these two judgments for some time now and for you to be free of this denseness will be a bit awkward at first. You may find yourself judging everyone and everything as judgment is leaving you. You feel it as it goes and you may even begin to see it grow stronger *in* you. This is simply you holding on to the old and it responding. Don't worry. You will lose it soon.

You must remember that *transformation* takes time. You are *"becoming"* while in the same body you chose to be born in. You are literally transforming a dense physical form into a service station of light. This form will be capable of restoring and regenerating on its own. This form will be used by God to rise into birth for a second time. This form will literally transform and become a way station for you. When you begin to travel inter-dimensionally you will know how to enter and leave form at will. Form will not die on you, form will work with you. This is the miracle of the transformation. You are creating a new level of body while still in body.

You will begin to understand more as you see the subtle changes in and throughout your body. You will begin to notice little changes that appear to be little sores or maybe little tensions. This is pain and ugliness leaving your body. Pain and ugliness (or the belief in ugliness) have created hatred and anger for the body. Most of you do not *realize* how angry you are at you, for not being tall, or handsome, or beautiful, or brilliant, or perfect. This, of course, is the illusion we are now dissolving.

Can you imagine being perfect? Can you imagine being everything that is right and good? This is what you will have when you let go of judgment and belief in right/wrong, good/bad. You will be the most handsome, the most beautiful, the most intelligent. You will not know discontent as you will not *judge* anything as other than perfect. Not only will you find all perfect, you will see *all* – absolutely everything as perfect, and you won't even think twice about it, because you will simply know that it is what God created and God is love not fear.

So, I wish you to know that you may stumble and go backward in your thinking as you release the programming that judges everything as good or bad, but this step backward is actually just you *seeing* what you are, as what you are transforms into the next level. What you are is an illusion. What you truly are, is love and love is perfection.

❧

Now I will tell you a story. Once upon a time in a land far away, you were born. It was a simple land and you knew it would be because you chose it for its simplicity.

Then one day you began to grow and see this land as much more. There became the idea of owning the land and even conquering it. You however, had never wanted so much to conquer it as you wanted to own it. You began to grow bigger and bigger and as you grew you wanted to own more and more land. You saw yourself as powerful and you gave what you could to assist those who were not so powerful. As you began to know more and more about yourself, you began to lose your "idea" of power. You now saw that power and strength both are within you and to be powerful with ownership is simply to *claim* your hold on the material world.

As you began to realize your true potential you began to give up ownership and hold only what could easily go. If you could, you simply purchased what you were not attached to, so you could easily let it go. This became your new strength. In the letting go of, you were being born to a much higher vibration. When you began to let go of your hold on property, your property no longer held you down.

This is the end of my story.

⚜

Now is the most important part of this book. I am going to tell you about God. God is not as you believe him to be. God is not a big voice or a big being who manifests before you. You *create* all manifestations and visions of God so as to attain a relationship with your own God-self. It is not so much that God does not manifest, but God does not separate into manifestations. God is whole and complete and God is *all* voices and all created forms.

When Liane heard my voice she *knew* that God was talking to her because God was *using* her to manifest. God does not manifest without permission. God does not control matter. God simply requests to arrive or come through, and you grant or do not grant permission. God is not the only energy who requests permission to enter you or your world. It is widely known how you on this plane have total control over your plane by free will choices. Because of this you will be very nice to whomever you trust and very upset with whomever you don't trust. Because of this it is most important to come to you and ask nicely and to gain your trust. You are almost barbaric to be as hostile and unforgiving as you are. I am not judging you; I am simply showing you where you now stand in the overall picture. You are not exactly easy to communicate with, because of your superstitious minds and your lack of awareness. Therefore, I came to Liane on a level she could relate to. She believed in a God in heaven and so I gave her what she could and would allow. Now she can *allow* more and I will give her what she will now *allow*.

Do you see how this works? It is all up to you. You may be told only what you are willing to receive. If you are told greater than you are ready for, you will run and hide like little superstitious natives. You have not evolved so greatly that you do not still carry huge amounts of fear. Your fear will keep you locked in to a reality that is so far from the truth that you may never see the truth. Let everything be true and you may find your truth among everything. Don't block! Don't fight over right and wrong. Don't be only one way and not the other. Go both ways. Allow polarities to merge, to cross over, to blend. You will find some semblance of truth running through everything.

Don't close your minds. Don't be uninformed about who you are. Be informed of all possibilities.

Knowledge cannot harm you. Only not knowing can drive you deeper into your fears. You are now on a very big journey within. You will begin to discover how you are God and how I am *in* (not outside of) you. You will begin to see how all is created by you in the blink of an eye. If you don't like what you are currently creating change it by changing your mind. Change your mind by reprogramming it. It is full of old memories that say, "Do not trust." Reprogram with memories for your future that say, "I am the light. I fear nothing. I am the light. I am nothing." As you become nothing you will become nothing but light.

❧

When you begin to know who you are you begin to assess your own value structure. You are not valuable in this world if you believe you are nothing. If you do not have money and you believe it is due to your own ignorance, you are creating judgment against you. You are also creating pain in your own consciousness by judging you for this situation. Now, why would you judge you for not owning paper and coin? Is it perhaps because you base your trust and security on paper and coin?

If that were true, you would only need paper and coin to make all your unhappiness go away. If paper and coin are so valuable and you have no value without them, you will of course become nothing (no identity, no ego, no popularity, no fun) without them. Without your security and your trust *in* you, you have nothing. Take *you* out of your money and put you back in you. You give so much power to having or not having money that you drain your own energy and put it into money. If you put half the time and energy into your own God-self that you currently put into making money, you would ascend in no time. This is what I wish you to do. I wish you to spend your time and your energy on you, not on them, not on creating wealth. If you truly wish to give, give to yourself and don't give to yourself by buying for yourself and creating more debt. Give to you by allowing you to simply be and by allowing you to *know* who you are and how you fool yourselves into situations you don't really want.

When you begin to know who you are you will also know how you create your reality and why you do not belong in someone else's reality without permission. It is not that you barge into another's space so much as it is you trying to take over and fix others. You cannot fix them, you can only fix you. You are putting your energy into fixing them and it takes all of you to change someone else. If you give all of your energy to someone else, you get exhausted and drained. When you become whole by drawing back out of other people's lives and realities, you will feel better. You will feel your strength and your energy return to you.

If you do not wish to live in your own reality you may change who you are and your reality will change as you change. So far you are doing well with this. You are waking gradually and re-collecting parts of you. Recollection is the beginning. It is okay to remember all that you have done and all that you have believed. It all changes when you look at it a second time in a new light. You may literally *transform* it by looking at it a second time from the view point of enlightenment. So, those of you who choose to forget and only move forward, I wish you to know that to *look* at all of you – whether you believe some parts to be ugly and painful or just sinful – to look will transform. Something as simple as reviewing your past from a new enlightened perspective will *change* how you see it now. In changing how you see it now, you also change how it was previously viewed as awful or painful, and it now becomes just something that occurred. This is *transformation* of *you* to *light*.

Let others use mind control and other methods that also have some effect, but for those who wish to *see* transformation take place "watch your own self – follow your own self – know your own self." Look at all your thoughts and your problems and your past. It is good to look at you and to review all in a new light. You grow in light simply by becoming aware. You are aware when you learn the truth about you. You cannot ignore your past and only *accept* and *allow* your present. *You* are *past, present* and *future*. Know it. Know you. Do not believe you can simply shut out your past and it will go away. Go into your past and allow it to be. Do not *ignore* or try to forget any part of you. Make only conscious choices from conscious knowledge of your total experience. *You* are all parts of you.

Allow all parts of you to come to the light. When you deny parts, be they past or present; you deny your light. Lighten up. Grow *in* the light and bring *all* of you to the light. Own it, for if you deny it you shut it off in a corner and it grows like an infection. It will eventually get your attention in some way. If you are sick you have ignored some part of you that must come to the surface. If you are angry and irritable you have ignored something that is trying to get your attention. If you are upset and feeling hurt you have a hidden secret you believe to be painful. Get it up and out of you. See it for what it is and you will be *accepting* part of you that you have been denying. You cannot bring something to the light if you continue to *deny* that it exists. Let it all be acceptable.

*W*hen you begin to see how you are not in you, you will begin to see how love is not in you. You are love. If love is not in, you are not in. When you know who you are, you begin to see you and accept you. As you see you, you begin to know how you feel and why you hurt you. As you grow, it will become apparent to you that you are not in your right place. When you learn more about you, you will learn more about your right place.

As you grow in strength and character you will see how all is created. Most of you are now in a position to see how your lives may have been a little bit of a mess. What you are not in position to see is how you decided to create that mess in the first place. So, as you grow you will see how and why you draw certain people into your lives. It is all to show you who you are. You are not always *direct* reflections of one another. Once in awhile you are being reflected to show someone a different view of themselves or even how it is to be opposite of them. At this time your reflection will be most helpful for you to see your own self, as you are buried so deeply *in* you. You are now in a position of seeing clearly how you are *inside,* and what you do to you.

If you see a fight it is you fighting within. If you push at another to change it is your *fear* that you will not change. As you grow in light you will learn how to see not only your own self as you truly are, you will also learn to see others as they truly are. You will no longer judge them as bad because it will simply be *your* reflection that is showing you your inner self. As you view your inner self you will come to know you better. Your inner self is you and you are very well aware of you on certain levels. It is only this unconscious you who does not see you as you truly are.

So; don't judge others for reflecting you to you.

You asked that they come into your life to do just that. You each have dysfunctional behavior that you hope to fix. This is why you constantly try to fix and control others, you wish to fix and control you. You want to heal and yet your old programming from the past is telling you to do this or react in a certain fashion to protect you. So you listen to this programming and it does not come from now it comes from your past. It must be changed. You must change in order to heal. When you are healed or fixed you will no longer feel the need to heal or fix others.

Most of you are dealing with multiple selves who are going in opposing directions. One self wants to heal and become light, the other self is happy to stay in its pain and dysfunction because it has grown to know pain and chaos as safe. It feels safe in chaos, so you now create chaos in your life and you judge you as being bad for creating chaos because your parallel personality wants peace. You are a split personality because you are light and dark. We are now transforming the dark into light and the dark has no choice but to move. Forced movement is often painful as it is *pulling* at the deepest roots of you. You may feel pain, confusion and discomfort as you lose your dark side or your fearful side.

As you begin to know you a little better you will begin to see how you do not know who you are at this point in time. This is self-discovery. As you *move* into your bright new future you will see how and why situations occur that trigger your fear. And what is fear? It is anger, irritability, hopelessness, anxiety, stress, pain, loneliness and much more. Fear is the dysfunction. Fear is the one who is afraid and will not change out of resistance. Fear is the blocking of light and fear is the blocking of love.

You may not see love without seeing the light. Love and light are one. Without love there is no light and without light there is dark. So; if you wish to see the light of love, you must change or switch-over to view love. You may view love by releasing all fear or pain. You may release pain through your enema on an energy level, and you may release pain through your belief system. See pain for what it is. Know how you created it to protect you, by seeing how you decided to block your growth in order to *protect* your hold on you. Your fear is stifling you and you are choking to death on something you created to protect you.

You have a very great ability to fool you. You think you are one thing but you are another. You believe you are love; you are actually preventing love by resisting love. You resist love because you believe love hurts. Love does not hurt. Love does not cause pain. Only your belief that love is dangerous has created so much pain regarding love. Love is pure. You are pure. We must empty you of your belief in pain. When you begin to trust you again you will begin to let go of your need to protect you from danger. You began to mistrust you because you got you into some situations that this conscious you did not understand. This conscious 'you' is suppose to be dumb and blind in order to *allow* you to create at this level. If this conscious you were not dumb and blind you would never have gone into fear, because it is impossible for light to enter dark without transforming the dark to light.

So now, you are beginning to wake up and no longer be dumb and blind. What happens when you wake up? You begin to see the truth. What happens when you see the truth? The game is over. No more playing in the illusion because you will dissipate the illusion. You will take the cover off. No more silly games with yourself. No more playing at being the opposite of God. You are God with a mask on and you are fooling no one but your own self.

Once you begin to see how you have hidden in this illusion you will begin to see how you do not wish to continue with this game. You came to play a game. You came to win. Now you have won repeatedly from the game and you are addicted to it. Let the game go, leave it alone. You are going home.

❧

So far you are being pulled in one direction. That direction is up! In order to rise you must let go of all past belief in pain, or ugly, or wrong or bad, or judgment. If your life looks awful at this point in time, it is due to the fact that you are letting go of these beliefs. You are rising up and as you rise they rise to the surface. You are seeing the stuff that has held you down for centuries. It is not hard to get rid of it, but it is difficult to hold on to it.

As you begin to rise, you will see significant changes in you. You will feel like you are learning and growing in awareness and yet you will re-experience old hurts and misunderstandings. You continue to replay your old systems of belief until you are ready to let go of them. Nothing changes in your life without your willingness to see it differently. You will change old patterns and old hurts simply by remembering how you first judged this situation as hurtful. Once you get to the original pain you can see all differently.

Many have been abused and do not consciously remember. Do you not trust men or women in your life? Did your parent or relative say "I love you" then punish you in some fashion? Were you mistreated for being small and available? Often this is the case. It is much easier to kick a small dog when you are angry than it is to kick a horse. Many people are out of control on this planet. Anger and pain are in the driver's seat and anger and pain must release. Most often a child is abused in some fashion, only because the child is available and smaller than a full grown adult who can and will fight back. Children are taught to obey adults and are confused and often submissive.

Many children at this time are growing in anger and fighting back. This is evolution. Your dysfunctions evolve as well as the rest of you. You are facing your own pain and anger when you see your angry and well armed youth killing, stealing, and carrying weapons. It is all you reflecting back at you. You are so deep in your own conflict of right and wrong that you do not see how it is all you. As you begin to see how you are hurt you will begin to forgive. You will forgive you for *believing* how awful you are. If you were mistreated as a child you were led to believe that you deserved it for whatever reason. This leads you to mistrust people and to protect yourself from further pain. You may be protecting yourself in many ways and if you continue, your walls of protection will be so thick that love will never find you. When you protect and guard yourself against anything you cut off the natural flow of everything to you.

You want to know why your lives are not working and I suggest you look within to your own frightened child. You cannot ignore any part of you be they past or future, because they are all here right now, in your present. It is all you. All time is right now. This instant is all you have. Don't leave parts of you in the dark; bring all of you home to the light. Now, for those of you who have childhood issues, I am going to suggest a book. It is titled *Homecoming* and is written by John Bradshaw. It will help you *see* how there is more to you at this moment than the adult you see. My pen has not yet read this book but I highly suggest it to her also.

So; read this book and learn about you. You can never learn too much about you because *you* are the unexplored universe. Remember when you discover who you are and how you got to be you, or this particular you with this particular belief system, that *you created it all* for a very good reason. No judgments please. Know who you are by looking at all aspects of you. It is time to no longer *fear* the past nor the future. It is okay to own what you are and then hand it over to God. Love it and let it go. Let God take over for you.

⁂

So far you are beginning to see how you create your world in order to prevent invasion by others. You are protective of your surroundings and this is why you arm yourselves. You wish to protect what is yours and you do so out of a belief that something or someone is going to harm you. So; how did you get to this point? Who harmed you in the first place and allowed you to reinforce your belief in evil or unkindness? When you begin to see why or how you developed your need for security you will see how you got you into pain. When you can let go of the need to protect yourselves from anything, you will be free.

It is not always protection that creates the illusion of safety. Sometimes it is safety that creates the illusion of fear. Sometimes when you believe you are safe and someone comes along to push into your safety zone you begin to mistrust everyone. You thought you were safe at home, or safe with a loved one, or safe with family members. But, it seems that your safety was violated and it was not your fault, but no one saved you or protected you from this situation. Maybe you developed a *belief* that your parents or parent did not protect you, so now you do not trust adults, even though you are an adult now. You may fear your boss or believe he is not fair with you. This could be your belief that your parent was harmful or just plain neglectful.

You will begin to see how everything in your adult life is connected to everything in your childhood. Why? Because you are all of you, not just this you, in this moment. You transform all of you by bringing all of you to the light. Do not abandon you. Do not leave part of you in the dark. You are all. All is you. Now; when you begin to rediscover your childhood programming you will become more *aware* of your actions and reactions. You will begin to see why certain people or certain issues "push your buttons" and get you all riled up. It is all connected to your past which is actually in the present with you. You are in this moment – all of you. You are not in a past or a future. The future is here now and the past is here now.

Once you begin to see how your life is one continuous line from top to bottom, you will see how you run up and down not side to side. As you go up you pull the weightier parts up with you. This is the old method and takes a great deal of mental power. For my students, I suggest you look at your weightier parts in order to transform them into light. After transformation, instead of pulling downward as you move up, they will now *assist* in your rise. The only reason you have any problem going "up" is resistance pulling you down. This makes the rise a real taffy-pull. I highly suggest that you get in touch with all parts of you and *allow* all parts of you to heal and then *watch how fast you go up!*

❧

*H*ow are you this morning? Great! Now I wish to teach you about God. God is good. God is light. God is forever. God is you! You will never end because God has no ending and no beginning. God is this universe and all other universes. Nothing ever ends. Things change. People change. Life changes. Nothing dies. Nothing ends. There is no ending for anything. If you burn it up it continues in another form. If you shoot it, it continues in another form. If it looks to you like it's gone it simply has left this dimension. If you are sitting in a room and you no longer see your friend who was just there, he or she has simply left that room. Do not believe in endings because everything is *evolving* into something else. There are no exceptions. Science will learn and so will Physics.

So; as you begin to see how nothing ends you will begin to see how there is no need to fear... not ever. The force will always be the force. The force is not only with you it *is* you. So, I suggest you begin to respect yourselves a little and observe in a new perspective. You don't end — ever! No one ends. No one dies. There are no dead war victims. There are no dead babies. You are just upset because they are not visible to you. You never lose anyone. You never lose, period! There is no such thing as loss. Everything will *change* to something else. If your home burns down with relatives in it, it will all come back in another form. No one goes away. Everything stays, but you simply can't see it.

When you begin to evolve you will see how this works. You too will disappear, only when you are evolved, you will have the ability to return if you so desire. Now; I wish to break this to you gradually and gently. Those who leave your planet are not always anxious to return. Once you are out of the dense pull, you do not always wish to reincarnate. For you who stay, you believe it is good fun. For those who leave and don't wish to return it is not their choice of a great vacation spot. It is up to each individual. Believe it or not, there are many areas in creation that are much more *evolved* and much more *loving* and have greater *peace*. Not everyone wishes to *hold* on to the earth plane.

If you know someone who wishes to go, let them. It is not wrong to want peace and harmony. At this point in time it is most difficult to find on your planet. Why do you judge those who kill themselves so harshly? Is it maybe your own fear of being the only one left in a war zone? Do you fear being left behind and not have the insight to share that knowledge? Maybe you want out too, but you do not *realize* that you do. It is not wrong to die. It is not wrong to kill yourself, so stop teaching this nonsense.

∾⁕∽

*M*ost often you are unable to control your destiny. This too is illusion. You are in complete control and complete denial of this ability. So far you only use part or a fraction of your creative abilities. You are God. You *are* the creators of heaven and earth. You are the one who molds life and creates storms and finds the stars and insists you know nothing about such things. You are the being who began it all by stopping the process of creative force. You simply began to withdraw your intention. You began to remove your belief in being God in order to show yourself how you can be or not be. You had a game with yourself and now you are *be*-coming again. You are becoming God inside of the original *idea* that you are not God. God is alive and *in* you, you simply choose to *believe* that God is outside of you. Your *belief* creates your reality.

I write through Liane. I have told you and I have told Liane that I now possess her body. She has shown herself signs that prove this to her, so she is now adaptable to me. She is like putty in God's hands. I create her life and she knows it and *accepts* it. Oh, she gets upset from time to time, but mostly she is pleased and so much more at peace than in her past. She *felt* me in her. She *believed* I possessed her and she became mine. She is learning to change her life and how she views all. You too will see how it is to be possessed by God; to give up total control. To *allow* others to have power over you is simply one way of giving up your control over them. If you are a control freak, as Liane once was, the fastest way to lose control is to put yourself in a living situation or work situation where you have no say. It will create and recreate any anger you may have stored in you from childhood. It will erupt to the surface as you are faced with your dilemma of how to survive and still be you, when you have no control over those you live with or work with. You answer to them.

This is one of your main fears from childhood. Everyone was your boss. You had little or no say in your household and in where you lived, or moved to, or what time you ate dinner, or what you ate for dinner. This created a feeling of being trapped in a situation. This is a very big *fear* in all of you. To be trapped and have no control really pushes your buttons. Therefore, the best way to bring these fears to the surface is to go into entrapment.

If you do not like where you are, move on. As a child you do not know that you may leave if it doesn't feel good, so you are all programmed to stay and take it. Now; I wish you to *realize* that you always have choices and you are never trapped. You may not like your choices, but you must know that you do have free will. If you do not like someone, get out. If someone overrides your will and simply ignores the fact that you have feelings and you are God – move. Leave and find your right place. If it feels good, stay. If it feels bad, go. If you choose to work out lessons and change how you see it – stay. If you choose to not see it differently and go, it is your choice. If you choose to stay and see it differently, it is your choice. You cannot lose. This is free will at work. You gave yourself free will and it is your gift to use. Stop pretending to be trapped. You may come in, you may go out. You are free. If you really want to leave you will. It's easy. Take one foot and put it in front of the other foot until you are out the door. Now, I suggest you try this simple method of getting out of your trap.

❧

Now and then you become upset over who is with you and who is against you. You begin to consider yourself as wrong if others do not agree with you. You are not wrong. You are simply finding your own center. You will begin to stop judging you when you begin to let go of right or wrong. As you begin to let go of right and wrong, you will have a great deal of confusion. Most of what you believe to be right will now be seen as simply *your* choice. And of course, what you begin to see as good, will now wipe out all wrong. So, as you begin to see the good in all things, you will be very unsure of your position, simply because it is a new position. You will shift from moment to moment. You will be flexible in your view point and yet uncertain of your view point.

Do not judge this new you. Allow you the time

needed to balance. When you balance you will become calm and you will know that it really does not matter what you say or do, because you are all going to the same place eventually. That place is awareness; God; love; peace; light. So, as you grow in love you grow in God. It is okay to believe in good and let go of your belief in bad. You have believed in evil for so long that it is a little difficult to get you to switch over to good. You still believe in danger, and pain, and wrong, and soon you will see only good, and heaven, and rightness of all creation; not because creation has changed, but because you have changed. And how did you change? By not accepting evil as the cause of creation.

When you begin to accept love or God as your creator, you begin to *see* only love or God in every *created* incident. Nothing is evil or bad, so you will see nothing but Good or love or God's creation. When you stop your own personal judgments you will feel so much better. Your judgments make you sick and I am here to heal you. Once you learn that you are not alone in this, you will drop your pretense that life is so awful. *Everything that occurs or does not occur on this planet is good.* Stop making it into something it is not. You are simply confused and totally unconscious. Wake up to what you are doing. You are condemning without *awareness*. You are simply pointing a finger and screaming "bad." It is not bad. It is not wrong. You are out of balance and seeing through distorted vision. You must balance in order to see good. If you insist on labeling everything as bad, or wrong, or dangerous, how do you expect to *ever* see love?

❧

*W*e are now moving into a time of great change. This change is to be reflected in your world and is *in* you. You are becoming God. You are changing your perception and learning that you *are* your own creator. As we move along in this new generation of love we will see a great deal of chaos. This chaos is to be transformed into light. Chaos is simply disorganization. Most of you are in a state of overwhelming uncertainty and you do not realize that you are simply reflecting change.

As you begin to become more and more of your true identity you will release more and more chaos and disorder. You will begin to seek peace and harmony, and in the seeking of peace and harmony you will draw peace. You are now at a point in your creation that is most unlikely, as it is not conducive to harmony. As you begin to vibrate at a softer and yet faster rate you will slough off all that is no longer representative of your new vibration. You are now growing *in* light and light moves quite rapidly. You will also notice that light penetrates the darkness as well as the liquid forms of earth.

When you begin to move into light you begin to transform into what you are now believing. If you believe in peace you *become* peace. If you believe in chaos you become chaos. You will transform you by your beliefs. Your beliefs are programmed into you by society, by creation as you understand it, and by what you have been taught. Now is a time of unteaching. This is when we take off all those layers of protection you once used in order to be safe from you. You will no longer hide from you. You will come face to face with you and you will *know* who you are and how you created it all simply by believing in it. You are the one who put you outside of God by creating separation. You chose to leave in order to experience unconsciousness. You have been *out* now for some time. It is time to come to. It is time to wake up from your unconscious state and to know how you are your own creator.

You are very much a part of God because you are God masquerading as what you now *believe* you to be. So; what do you believe you to be? Do you know who you are? Do you know who you believe you are? You are no longer blood and flesh, as I have taught you that you are thought. So, if you believe you are thought, you then begin to transform blood and flesh into thought. After you become thought you become energy, as thought moves as energy. After you move and think, you become transformed into light. After you *believe* you are light, you may accomplish anything.

It is not long now before you begin to trust and know you are light. You may learn who you are by peeling back the layers of belief that you carry. You once *knew* that you were God and in order to convince yourself you were not, you began to believe you had limitations. Now we are working our way back through these limitations in order to free you from them. As you release your belief in humanness and limitation, you will become *aware* of another identity that was once you. This is Godness. You chose to layer yourself with dense energy; because you were God and the only way to get God to forget he is God is to force him down with dead weight, or dense energy.

It's almost as though you, as God, drugged yourself to forget you are God to experience limitation. You as God experience nothing. You simply are. As human, you experience and even become the experience by taking it on as your own. Now I am teaching you to let go of your experience as you, by letting it come to the forefront so you may *release* it. You might even think of yourself as simply an experience; an experiment in time and space. You were created in order to create and for no other reason. God is and does out of being. There is no big reason. No mystery, no pretense greater than the one you perpetrate on you. You see; you are the God who went unconscious in order to become experience and now you are returning from this experience in time.

It is not such a big deal really. It is only because you do not wish to acknowledge your own knowledge that you cannot or do not understand. This too is your choice – to *experience* not knowing when you are literally the knowledge of all. You know it and you are it – you are the universal consciousness and unconsciousness all at the same time. Quite a game you play with yourself isn't it?

❧

*A*s we begin ascension we begin to notice changes in ourselves. We begin to see how we have clung to stuff that weighs us down. We also see how we have clung to people who weigh us down. You cannot do the rising for another. You may try lift-off with someone you care for on your back, but the results will be a struggle to lift-off. You will find it difficult to do your work and their work. No one can fix you but you. No one can fix them but them.

Desire must be in place before one learns to lift-off. Then it takes a very high frequency vibration to project into fourth dimensional reality. If you are trying to lift-off while carrying others, you will not achieve your fourth dimensional belief. You must let go of those whom you are tied to, or stuck to out of honor, or even addicted to. Many of you have *attached* yourselves to people who are similar to your parents in some way. They bully you, or protect you, or yell at you, or abuse you as your parents once did, so now you feel *secure* with them. I know that in your society you teach that alcoholic parents raise a child who either becomes alcoholic or marries an alcoholic. This is also true for abusive parents. If you were abused or ignored, you will grow up and *attach* yourself to an adult who either abuses you or ignores you. You will repeat your childhood, because you are programmed by childhood experience to accept this person as a parental figure who loves you and protects you from the big bad world.

Even if a parent was physically abusive you will return to this cycle of abuse in some form. Why? Because it is security of home and protection from *outside* hurt. You return to the nest, so to speak. You return to what you knew best and where you learned to function. If you were silenced about the abuse, you will find yourself with people who don't really want you to speak up about your pain. When you begin to release your pain and your abuse you will freely move on to another level of security. When you do so, you will encounter people who are vibrating and healing as you are.

As you begin to move up this ladder of success you will *see* more and more beauty in life. You will no longer feel the *need* to focus your attention on only the "good" in life because the "good" is all that you will see. You will find it very difficult to see the bad in anything. When the pain goes, it will take with it the mistrust you feel and your security will no longer lie in other people, or stuff, or money. Your security or safety will now be your own truth about you and who you are. You will no longer seek security as you now seek it, for it will simply be your own *knowledge*. Ignorance breeds fear. Fear is the cause of all hurt and dysfunction. You may change fear to love simply by accepting what you fear and no longer judging it as bad or wrong. Only judgment stands between you and heaven on earth... your judgment!

❧

*W*henever you change you create stretching and growth. Stretching often is accompanied by pain or inflexibility. Often inflexibility is felt in the neck area. Your neck will tell you if you are up-tight or inflexible. Neck soreness or stiffness is often a sign of not wanting to see what you are looking at. Most of you will find that to look at your own fears is probably the most uncomfortable part of you. You wish to see who you are, however you are not willing to face up to who you are. You judge you at every turn and this is simply a sign of how you dislike and mistrust you. Your dislike and mistrust of others is nothing when compared to your dislike and mistrust of you.

You see, you *blame* you for everything that has ever occurred in your life or lives. You blame you – only you believe that you don't. You believe that you blame others and often you judge yourself for blaming them, but in actuality, this is simply a reflection of how much and how often you blame you for everything that you believe hurt you in some way. You believe that you made some big mistakes either spiritually or mentally and this is why you judge you so harshly. Oh, you don't know of this part of you yet, but I thought I would let you know that it's there *in you*.

Now; if you see others as having done something bad to you, I want you to know that this is simply a *reflection* of how you believe you did wrong for you or to you. You all carry this defect called judgment. Watch how you see life and you will know how heavily or lightly you judge you. This will also tell you how heavy or light you are. You are now coming to a place in your evolution that is most remarkable. It is the present. You are bringing your past into your present and creating a bright new future for you. You are bringing *all* of you to the surface in order to change whatever future was or is in place. You may change you and all past and future reflections change. It is as simple as taking a new path or new direction in experience.

I want you to begin to *experience* light. I want you to see from the light not from the dark. I want you to wake up and come home. You are out-of-place-energy, and it is time to return to the center. You are my mind and soul. You are literally a dream in motion. You *are* the creation of God. How can you judge you for being less than God? There is no way to be less than God. You can only *pretend* to be something less and this is the game you play.

Wake up now and know the truth. You have been lying to yourself and others for so long that you *believe* your own lies. Stop lying and begin to accept the truth that God is dreaming of an experience and it is not bad nor is it wrong. It simply is!

*W*henever you begin to have doubts about your own sanity you are changing. Your sanity is based on how you view your environment and how you *relate* within this environment. Your relationship to everything changes when you begin to rise up. You no longer *expect* to have it your way and you no longer judge others as wrong for having it their way. Mostly, you simply begin to accept that life is good no matter what comes to you. You then begin to see the good in all. As you begin to see the good in all, you begin to know how you are good and not evil. As you begin to know how you are good and not evil you begin to *allow* you to be, regardless of what you draw into your life.

Now we have you being love and *accepting* your own good. It's actually very simple. See the good in all situations and you get the good in all situations. If you have it your way it is good. If you don't have it your way, it is good. In this type of a situation you cannot lose. If you get what you want it is great, and if you don't it's great also.

So, how can you get to this level of insanity? I suggest you try believing it first. As you believe so you receive. So, let go of your fear regarding life and begin to see all as a big gift. Look for the gift in every situation. It may be as simple as a flash-back to childhood to show you where your fears lie, or it may be a way to force some of your own pain and insecurities to the surface. When you see pain, know that it is coming "up" in order for you to heal. Allow pain to surface and allow you to let it be expressed. Do not judge you for expressing pain. You are expression. Expressing is what you do.

When you begin to express pain do not judge you for doing so. You are beginning to *feel* your own inner self heal and if you have great pain it is best to let it flow, all energy is meant to flow, even pain. Do not stifle pain. Let it come up and express itself. You are not bad to have pain. You all have it to some degree and those of you who are now healing are looking into the face of evil to *see* what evil really is. Only evil will show you evil. It contains all dense energy as it is fear. Look at fear. There really is nothing to fear but what you are, and you are afraid to look at what you are because what you are frightens you. This is the biggest denial you have. Denying your own self is your problem. There are no problems that cannot be solved by simply looking into you to see what makes you tick.

You are so out of control with fear that you fear you. You do not wish to wake up because *you* believe you to be so awful that you would be horrified to really see your own pain. You are not horrible, you are simply afraid of you. You fear you. You created evil to block you from your own good. You then convinced yourself that you could have good without loving you. So, you decided to call relationships and cars and jobs and houses and money *good*. You are no longer considered good. Even when we discuss receiving, you do not jump up and down with joy over receiving a relationship with you. You do, however, jump up and down over receiving a gift of a relationship with someone else. Why can't you love you? Why can't you be the gift in your life? Why must the gift be money, or relationships, or travel? How far at the bottom of your chart or scale have you put the *value* of you? I think you have a great deal of work to do on *you*. When you can learn to desire you over money, jobs, relationships, boats, houses and the big dream, you will have moved *you up* in your own status quo. You will no longer require jobs, people, money and stuff to validate you. You will know that you are *all* there really is. It is okay to quit your job. It is okay to let go of everything because everything is what you already are, you are simply *afraid* to look.

Now and then you begin to know who you are and how you got here. You begin to see how you may have created your own life as well as this universe you live in. When you begin to fully understand how you are a part of everything and how everything is a part of you, you will know how you fit in. You are no longer part of the whole. You are the whole, in that you are the whole of your experience. Once in a great while you begin to see how you are not so bad. You are simply the creator creating and being misunderstood and even misquoted. When you begin to see how things truly are you will know shame.

You all have shame from being taught shame. "Shame on you" is taught often on your planet and each time someone tells you of shame you feel shame. Shame is pain and judgment that says you were bad or wrong to do this or that. Most shame comes from not obeying the rules. You know you are bad when you do not obey the rules of your society because everyone is very quick to tell you how wrong you are. Did you ever wonder why you have such strict enforcement of rules? It is to keep you in line; to keep you on a line and to keep you from freely expressing your true nature. Why? Because, if you cut your lines, you may just surprise you and everyone else by doing something unusual and even frightening.

Yours is the dimension of fear through control, limitation and restriction. Don't dare to talk back or even speak your truth or the moral majority will pounce. Why? Because *you* set it up this way to keep you in line. Why? Because *you* are afraid of your own ideas and thoughts, and especially your ability to do whatever you feel like doing. There are no chains that hold you prisoner that were not put in place by you for your own protection. You have created your world of limitation and restraint to keep you from being and knowing that you are God.

Now you may let go. Now you may flow with creation and know that you are totally free in every way. No one to fear, no limitations, nothing to fear, no death, no more lying to your own self. Fly free! Know that you cannot – absolutely cannot – do wrong. It is impossible for you to be wrong. There is no such thing. It was all a trick you played with yourself and now the trick is over because you are no longer buying into it. You are good and every move you make is acceptable. Now; I know this frightens you, but you must begin to accept the truth of your infinity. You are infinite. You have no beginning and no end. You are limitless instead of "limitation." You chose to see the reverse side of you. It's not such a big deal to look at the lie and begin to believe it. Now we must look at the truth in order to believe it once again.

You came a very long way from truth and now you sit in the dark and you preach how unsafe it is. *You*, my dear sweet child, are sitting in an illusion that you created. *Open your eyes.* You are sitting there with your eyes shut tightly and telling me the truth as you see it. When you shut your eyes you only see what your mind creates for you to see. *Open your eyes!* It is not too painful and the light is bright, but your eyes will adjust gradually and then you will be able to look around at the truth. This world that you live in was created in the mind of God. It is not God. It is simply God's imagination at work. Look into you and you will see only what is in you. Look out at the world and you will see a reflection of what is in you. Look at the light and you will see how you are God and nothing else exists except the fact that you are dreaming.

You do not create light out of fear, judgment, lies, darkness and illusion. You create light by letting it "be." Let everything be and judge nothing. Can you do this? Can you spend an entire day judging nothing that you see? Knowing only that this or that situation is occurring in absolute perfection. Do not judge bank robbery, or murder, or abuse. Can you? I know this is not what you have been taught, however what you have been taught got you here and now you are screaming to get out! I will lift you out if you will just "lighten up" enough to let me pull you up. If you hang on to old beliefs you are stuck in them. Let go and rise up! You can do this. This is part of your plan.

You left God by pretending to not be God. Now you are returning by agreement to be God once again. You see, your mind is so powerful that you become a dancer by believing you are and even a plumber by knowing you are. Now become God by knowing you are. Become good instead of bad by knowing you are. And live in peace instead of war by letting war be peace. Nothing is too difficult for you. You are all that is and all that ever will be. If you are so vast you will have little difficulty *believing* that you are the goodness of this planet. "No one else is," you say. If you choose to see everyone as bad, you get bad. However, if you choose to see everyone as love expressed, you get love. The choice is yours as it always has been.

❧

When you begin to wake up you may have a big headache. You have slept for so long that you may become sluggish and a little disoriented. As you begin to clear more and more of your old belief system you may feel exhausted and emotionally drained. It is all part of change. It is all part of letting go. You must remember that layers are literally being peeled away and a new you being exposed. You are not to judge you for being one of the first to wake up. Let the rest of the planet continue with daily activities. Your new daily activity is to peel. Peel off the old creation to allow way for the new.

Most of you are not even aware of the fact that you are peeling. You think you're just going through a rough time. It is not easy to see what is not visible to you. You will know more about you by learning to communicate with your soul. If you have not begun to communicate directly with your inner being how do you ever expect to know who you are and how you are waking? It is not yet time for those of you who do not wish to wake, but for those who do and are, your time grows near. The more you can communicate with your own Godness the more you propel into your future of love and peace.

You may find that you no longer create disease for yourself, however you are often light headed, dizzy, spacey or sluggish. This is all part of clearing away the debris. Think of it as sweeping a very dirty floor that has not been touched in years. As soon as you begin to clean this floor, the dust and debris begin to fly. If you use a shovel you may get there faster and you will be pulling up big chunks of old, hardened debris off this floor. The debris is actually *attached* to the floor, so as you clear it of its old garbage it affects the floor. It may pull at the floor or it may pull up part of the floor with it. It depends on how strongly the floor and the debris have grown into one another.

If you pull up parts of your floor you must replace it with new flooring. This is what takes a little more time, and so at times you may feel as though this cleaning out process will never end. This of course is not true. The process of cleaning you up is going to end as soon as you get to the bottom of what is causing your pain, and how you created the mechanics of judgment that created a painful situation in the first place.

If you never judged anything you would not carry pain. As it is now you judge everything as bad, i.e., weather, traffic, people, pollution, crime, religion, government, abortion, prison, wildness, craziness, illness, colds, sensitivity, insensitivity, divorce, teenagers, guns, violence, passivity, you name it, there is some way to judge it. So, judgment comes in and says this is awful or unfair. You then believe this judgment, and when this situation occurs in your life you already have judgment in place to tell you to *allow* it to be awful and get hurt by it.

Now; if there were no judgment in place and this situation were new for you, you would simply see it as an experience. Your attitude would be, "Oh my, isn't this interesting, something new for me to experience." And of course, because you are without judgment you are also without fear. So if this situation involves danger you would not respond from fear. You would only respond from within the moment or instant of this experience. It then becomes neither good nor bad, but simply an experience.

This is where you will all be at some point in your evolution. This is the truth of the universe – that "everything simply *is*," is the great truth. As you begin to notice how you are changing as you uncover your programming that taught you to judge, you will feel bewildered and upset at times. This is natural. It is all judgment coming to the surface to be released. Judgment in you is very, very strong. As you release it, it may tear at you where you are strongly attached to it. As it leaves, you may feel this tearing and you may feel the need for rest and seclusion from others. This is actually very good for you. As you begin to heal you will feel much more energy and the ability to function in and among others will return. Do not judge you for being in seclusion. You are simply healing and you need a nice private, quiet space to heal. Pretend you have had psychic surgery and *allow* you to rest. I know this is difficult in your motivation oriented world, but I suggest you give peace a chance by allowing you peace and quiet.

☙❧

So far it is not difficult to see how far you have come. You are strewn with memories and opinions and judgments concerning life and death. I want you to stop judging and begin to love and allow all creation to exist in its own way. I realize that this is a great deal to ask, but you will always be God and you will always be love and acceptance, so you might as well begin to know it and act it. You are one of the biggest and best and yet you put you down constantly. You *are* the creator and you judge your creations. You are harder on you because you believe you can do better and what you do not know is that you have achieved perfection. The goal was to go unconscious and you have. You have reached your goal and now it is time to go back home.

You will begin to see many different levels of creation as you return. You will see how you zigged or zagged to avoid injury or certain problems in the creation itself. These are your paths or your webbing that covers, or layers you. In order to get out here in this darkness and illusion, it was necessary to spin a web of lies and even to *wear* this webbing until you became it. This is what you now are. You are a vast, interconnected webbing system made up of your beliefs. These beliefs were concocted to get you lost in dense matter. These lies worked. You are lost and you believe these lies right down to believing that death, or leaving this planet is awful. You even believe that you are awful. Oh, you may not know it, because you separated yourself to the extent that you don't even know what you really believe. Quite a game of champions when you think about it.

So now we have you sitting, reading these pages, wondering what in the world I am getting at, all because you have lost your contact with you. You left on a mission and now you are out of touch with the part of you who sent you out. Well, guess what? You were smart enough to give yourself "free will" which overrides any of the silly rules you create along the way. You see, you knew it would be difficult to stay *down*. After all, you are light and light does not descend nor does it turn to darkness. Light is lifted up and light is energy without limitation. So now you have convinced yourself that you are not good enough to be God and the most amazing thing is that you actually believe this. This is the greatest lie of them all. I mean, you have taught yourselves to believe some pretty wild stuff, but this really tops them all! The creator has so effectively gone undercover that even when he is told who he is he won't believe it.

So; what am I to do? I am your other half and I wish you to return to consciousness and end this silly game you have created. Enough of the lies and judgments. Come back to the truth. The truth is light and the light will save you from going deeper into the lie. You may make your choice as to whether you wish to continue believing the lies that led you here, or you may choose to believe the truth and begin your return to the light. The choice is yours. You may ask to stay and not believe me or you may choose to rise up to your true status and *allow all creation to simply be*. This is your ultimate goal. Your goal was to get as dark as you could and then reverse this process by shedding light on it. You now have the opportunity to shed some light on a very dark situation. The darkness does not come from the creation of a situation. The darkness comes from the judgment held against a situation. Non acceptance blocks the flow and shuts parts of you down.

When you begin to see how you judge all and how you create vast amounts of pain through your judgments, you will wish to let go of judgment and return to love. Love feels better than judgment and love flows freely, whereas judgment is stuck. So, as always, it's your choice. Stay stuck or flow. You choose.

Now I wish to end this book and allow my pen a brief vacation before starting our next book, *See the Light*. I do hope you have enjoyed this series and I do hope you will show some interest in returning to the light. There is a great deal for you to learn yet in regards to your own abilities and your destiny. You are not so bad as you *believe* you are. Look at you through love and leave evil alone. He is not your right place. Judgment created evil to continue the lie. Come home to the truth that love is all there is. You really are imagining absolutely anything that you do not see as love-created. I know you have a lot to learn, but I think you are ready.

God's Pen

I first heard the voice of God in 1988. I was sitting in my back yard reading a book when this big booming voice interrupted with, "I am God and I will not come to you by any other name." I felt like the voice was everywhere – inside of me as well as in the sky around me. I was so frightened that I ran in my bedroom to hide.

This was not the first time that I heard voices. I had been communicating with my own spirit guide or soul for about a year. I guess my depth of fear regarding God, and all that he represented to me at the time, was just too much.

I spent two days trying to avoid the voice of God, which was patiently waiting for me to respond. By the second day I was exhausted from lack of sleep and decided to give in and talk with him. This turned out to be the greatest gift and best decision of my life.

The first book, *God Spoke through Me to Tell You to Speak to Him*, shows my evolution from communicating with my soul to communicating with the Big Guy. It took a couple years for me to be comfortable communicating with God. My fear of a punishing God was big! That has most definitely changed and I now think of God as my partner and best friend.

In the beginning the voice of God would wake me in the middle of the night and tell me it was time to write. He said I had promised to do this work (I assumed he was talking about the soul/spirit me). I would drag myself up to a sitting position and watch in amazement as my hand flew across the page, while I tried to keep up by reading what was being written.

It was always so much fun to wake up the next morning and grab my notebook to see what God had written during the night. After some time the voice stopped waking me and I became comfortable picking up my pen and writing for God first thing in the morning. I think in the beginning I had to be awakened while still semi-conscious from sleep so I wouldn't object too much to the information that was being channeled through me.

As I grew less and less afraid (and more trusting) of God, he was able to communicate greater information. Some of the information is quit controversial, but I felt it important to just let it be and not censor it. I present the writings here to you as they were given to me. I have edited a little (mostly the more personal information regarding myself) and I have used a pen name for privacy reasons. I asked God for a good pen name and he guided me to Liane which (I was told) in Hebrew means "God has answered."

At one point I became a little concerned about my sanity in all this, so I went to a hypnotherapist to find out what I was doing. Under hypnosis I saw this incredibly huge beam of light with a voice coming from within it. It was a giant "loving light" and felt so comforting and kind. It felt like that's where I came from. After that I stopped worrying about my sanity. If this is crazy, I think it's a very good kind of crazy to be….

In loving light, Liane

Loving Light Books

Available at:
Loving Light Books: www.lovinglightbooks.com
Amazon: www.amazon.com
Barnes & Noble: www.barnesandnoble.com

Also Available on Request at Local Bookstores